?WHAT

How to Start a
Creative Revolution
at Work

How to Start a Creative Revolution at Work

Dave Allan, Matt Kingdon, Kris Murrin, Daz Rudkin

CAPSTONE

First published 1999 by
Capstone Publishing Limited
Oxford Centre for Innovation
Mill Street
Oxford OX2 0JX
United Kingdom
http://www.capstone.co.uk

British Library Cataloguing in Publication Data
A CIP catalogue record for this book is available from the British Library

ISBN 1-84112-068-5

Typeset by
Sparks Computer Solutions Ltd, Oxford
http://www.sparks.co.uk
Printed and bound by
Wm Clowes Ltd, Beccles, Suffolk

This book is printed on acid-free paper

Substantial discounts on bulk quantities of Capstone books are available to corporations, professional associations and other organisations. For details telephone Capstone Publishing on (+44-1865-798623) or fax (+44-1865-240941).

We dedicate this book to the fabulous team at ?What *If!*,
who have joined the creative revolution.

Also to our partners,
Alice, Amanda, Emma and Ian.
Your support and tolerance was fantastic.

Thanks.

Acknowledgements
Special thanks to Des, Emma, Kathy and Suzi

Contents

Welcome to the Revolution   *xiii*

Creativity is the great leveller. There are few other areas of human activity in which we all start out so equal. So why are some people better at it than others? The difference is that some of us learn and practice creative habits while others do not. Discover the six behaviours of highly creative people – what do they do that's so different?

Creative Behaviour 1: Freshness   1

The first law of creativity is that the quality and uniqueness of stimulus in has a direct impact on the quality and uniqueness of ideas out. This chapter shows you how to fill your mind with freshness. Learn the four techniques of river jumping to break out of conventional thinking.

Creative Behaviour 2: Greenhousing 51

Greenhousing protects young ideas when they are at their most vulnerable and nurtures them into healthy growth. We've seen organisations and the individuals in them significantly increase the creative buzz of their working lives when armed with the greenhousing principles explained in this chapter.

Creative Behaviour 3: Realness 95

Realness at work means that you stop talking, sending memos and convening meetings and start actually *doing*. Understand how 'word-only zones' block creative behaviour and learn practical ways to unleash realness in your workplace. When you experience the creative rush that realness delivers – believe us – you will never go back!

Creative Behaviour 4: Momentum 127

How does it feel to be working on a project that has momentum? You can feel the positive buzz in the air. In this chapter you will learn how to dismantle the four barriers to momentum and replace them with passion, enthusiasm and emotional openness. We like to think of it as 'unreasonable urgency'. You can spot the energy and excitement a mile off.

Creative Behaviour 5: Signalling   171

Signalling is the fifth behaviour of highly creative people. Here we will help you develop awareness of the two states of business thinking and how to navigate between them. We will explain the use of visual, verbal and physical signals and we'll give you practical and priceless signalling tools for both one-to-one and group situations.

Creative Behaviour 6: Bravery   207

Why is it that we admire bravery so much in others but find it hard to be brave ourselves? Why do brave people never consider themselves brave? What are the barriers to bravery and how can we overcome them? You will find out here how to build the five steps to lasting bravery into your own personal bravery plan.

A Call to Arms   *239*

The creative revolution at work has already started. It's up to you whether you want to be part of it. You can start today!

Index   *243*

Welcome to the Revolution

'Innovation and creativity are vital to our growth'.

9/10 people we talk to strongly agree with this statement.

So practically, do you know how to practice and inspire creativity in your day-to-day life at work?

Ask this question and 9/10 people admit the answer is 'no'.

Why is this?

Doing it. Not talking about it

This book is about starting a creative revolution at work. But what sort of revolution?

Instinctively, we all know creativity at work is important. If creativity sees the commercial light of day, if it actually happens, that's innovation. And to most of us innovation means growth. To some extent, then, all our business futures depend on our ability to be creative at work.

Important stuff, but hardly new. We've been told about the need for innovation – about the need for a creative revolution – for years now. Not just in the press. Chairmen and CEOs regularly extol the virtues of innovation. For shareholders it's a message that falls on eager ears. What's missing in most cases is the practical follow-through. Companies keep talking about the 'why we need it' without the 'how are we going to do it?'

Why is this? Most businesspeople accept that innovation (and so creativity) is 'important', but it's rarely classified as 'urgent'. The bottom line benefits of a creative act may not be felt for one, two or even three years. This does not easily fit the short-term focus of modern business. Moreover, creativity is one of those 'easy to talk about but hard to do' activities. It can be intimidating. Many people put it on a pedestal. They shake their heads and say it's 'not for them'.

There are other convenient reasons not to engage with the practical nuts and bolts of creativity. There is always something else potentially more pressing. 'I need to get the core business sorted before I can even think about creativity.' 'If only I could recruit more people.' 'If only I had more funds.' 'I need more time to think.'

All of these factors mean it's all too easy to put creativity on the back burner – something to be addressed later. The trouble is there never is a 'right time'. If creativity is important to your business, the time to start is now.

This book contains everything you need to start a creative revolution in your organisation. It aims to demystify creativity at work by providing a series of tried and tested tools to get on and do something about it. It pushes beyond theory to give practical techniques that you can apply every day of your working life.

Why be creative?

We use the words creativity and innovation a lot in this book. These two words are often used as though they are interchangeable. To us, they mean different things. By our definition, creativity only becomes innovation when ideas become useful. In the business world, that means when a new product or service is launched, or starts to make money. Creativity is a behaviour; innovation is a process.

As Mark Twain observed: 'The man with a new idea is a crank until the idea succeeds.' For us, innovation is directly linked to creativity, but it is not the same thing. In business, the link is not always clearly understood. Creativity gives birth to new ideas but it is also essential for transforming those ideas into commercial reality. Creativity, then, is the behaviour that animates the innovation process.

Today, the business case for innovation is almost universally accepted. In recent years, company after company has tried to become more innovative to improve its competitiveness. But we believe it goes deeper than that.

As human beings, creativity is in our blood. It's as simple as that. Creativity is a skill we all have and can all enjoy. Whether it's inventing a new game with your children, painting your kitchen purple or landscaping your garden, we all recognise the joy and pride that comes from having an idea and making it happen. It's our ability to create, to make previously unseen connections, that really defines us as human beings.

Opposable thumbs have been very useful, but only because they have enabled us to make things. It is creativity that is Man's greatest – and most under-developed – skill. In business, it is a skill that is increasingly important. In the United States, for example, the Intellectual Property Association has estimated that the so-called creative sectors – chiefly communications, information, entertainment, science and technology – are already worth $360 billion a year, making them more valuable than automobiles, aerospace or agriculture.

But it's not just software developers and research scientists who require creative skills. Everything from problem-solving to process design, from strategy to customer service, requires creativity. Today, in every industry and at every level, companies are crying out for employees to be more innovative, more flexible, more imaginative, more motivated, more open to change. They want them to reinvent their jobs, their processes, their organisations, their working practices, and just about everything else you care to think of.

No matter how big or small the act of creativity, the principles behind it are the same. You might be seeking a step-change in the creative capability of an entire organisation, or organising a children's' party. It doesn't matter. We've observed that creative people approach these different tasks in the same basic way.

Two worlds

Every single one of us can be more creative. Creative behaviour can be learned. The problem is that many of us either don't feel like bringing our innate creativity to work with us, or the business unwittingly suppresses it.

We believe there are two worlds to business: a traditional analytical world; and a creative world where gut feel counts. Most large organisations have both, but they have much too much of the analytical world. There just isn't the opportunity for creative behaviours to take root and flower.

Our creative revolution doesn't advocate dismantling the traditional world of business – we think that world is fine most of the time. What we're saying is that when creativity is on the menu we need to jump into another world.

Ironically, the more successful companies become, the more they lose touch with their entrepreneurial roots. Over time, they develop systems that end up beating the life out of creativity. They get stuck in the analytical world, and find it harder and harder to step into the creative one. (How and why the entrepreneurial spirit dies with corporate growth is an important issue, and one that we will explore in the chapters that follow.)

Failure to navigate between the traditional world of 'analysis' and the world of 'creativity' not only compromises business growth, it also undermines personal growth and job satisfaction, reducing feelings of fulfilment through work. Shutting off creative behaviour denies ourselves part of who we are. Sure, we all come to work to earn money, but there is so much more to our motivations than that.

The creative revolution we advocate is about both corporate and personal fulfilment.

Why listen to us?

The authors are the four partners of a company called ?What *If!*, based in London, UK. Our mission is to help large companies that have become stale to recapture their inventive spirit.

The authors, from the left: Matt Kingdon, Daz Rudkin, Dave Allan and Kristina Murrin.

Fifty passionate souls work at ?What *If!* and since we started in 1992, we've been lucky enough to help shape the culture of some of the worlds biggest, fastest growing, and most profitable organisations. We have helped our clients invent new airports, beers, stores, toys, holidays, shampoos and even mortgages!

In that time, we have led hundreds of innovation projects and trained more than 5000 people all over the world in creative behaviour. Our intention has been to set up a unique way of working. We call it an 'inside-out culture'. Part of that culture is to try new things habitually. We have had some spectacular disasters and spectacular successes. As a result we have built up a vast store-cupboard of practical experience about what blocks innovation and how innovation really works. We have also found ways to kick-start and accelerate creative behaviour in organisations.

Constant experimentation allows us to keep pushing creativity deeper into the hearts of our clients' organisations as well as our own. In this business, forget theories. You can only teach creativity by doing creativity. Everything we learn about designing and running innovation projects feeds into what we teach in creativity workshops.

The second aspect of an 'inside-out culture' is that we try very hard to be what we teach. We have directly experienced all of the creative behaviours described in this book. We know that they work. We have seen the results when we introduce them to clients and when we practise them ourselves.

Why behaviours?

This book is about behaviour. It's all about being different and trying new and different things. Unlike the vast majority of business books, our challenge is not to change the way you think, it's to change the way you act. Focusing on behaviours, we have found, is the most effective way of inspiring a creative revolution at work.

Our experience is that people find it really hard to make dry theory come alive. But they can implement new behaviours. And adopting new behaviours affects the way you feel. You may not feel more creative straight away, but if you *behave* creatively, after a while you will genuinely feel your creative capacity increase. Believe us, this really works! If you've ever been out for the evening feeling low, but decided to put a smile on your face anyway, you will know what we mean. In a short time you find your mood changes. Your smile makes you feel more positive. Creative behaviour works in the same way. Behave creatively and you will feel creative.

So what do creative people do that's different? We have deliberately broken creativity down into six separate behaviours. In this way we hope to demystify it and make it accessible to everyone. At present, many people feel it is the preserve of a certain type of person. Simply telling people to be more creative doesn't help. But once you look at it in this unbundled way, creativity falls off its pedestal. It becomes easy to talk about, easy to practise and even to measure.

Looked at in this way, creativity is like any other sort of activity. It becomes something we can all get on and do.

Our creative revolution involves adopting six specific behaviours:

- freshness;

- greenhousing;

- realness;

- momentum;

- signalling; and

- bravery.

These are the behaviours that we have observed and experienced in highly creative and high performing teams. Our research in this area supports this. A recent study we carried out suggests that these behaviours are a key difference between inventors and managers in large companies. We surveyed 500 middle managers from large multinationals, and 500 inventors (people who have patented at least one idea and get a significant proportion of their income from their own inventions). We found that the inventors were significantly more likely to exhibit the six behaviours than their managerial counterparts. The specific behaviours where inventors exhibited the greatest dissonance with managers were greenhousing (15 percent more), realness (21 percent more) and bravery (17 percent more).

These results probably won't surprise you. At some level, we all know that creative people spend their time in slightly different ways to other people. As we examine each of the six behaviours, we are also sure that many of our observations will resonate for you. That's because they tap into intuitive knowledge that you already possess. Whether you choose to release that creative potential is, of course, up to you.

Whatever your job, whatever you do, the principles can be tailored and applied to how you work. But in the end, the value you extract from this book will be in direct proportion to your willingness to take a leap and try out some of these behaviours. It's really up to you. The fact that you are reading this book suggests that you are open to a new way of working, one that releases your creative potential.

Welcome to the revolution.

Is this you?

Your days have a predictable pattern to them. You take the same route to work, read the same newspaper or listen to the same radio station every day.

Most of the people you spend time with are from similar backgrounds.

You rarely try new things, meet new people, or visit new places because it's easier to stick to what you know.

You are so busy that you tend to settle for the first good solution to a problem.

You suspect that many of your ideas could easily be copied by your competitors.

You worry that the ideas you and your team come up with are incremental rather than revolutionary.

Fresh: Other, different, not previously known or used.
Source: *Oxford English Dictionary*

Freshness: The deliberate organisation of new and different inputs and stimulus to your work life to provoke alternative perspectives.
Source: ?What *If!*

Why freshness matters

Next time you finish a brainstorm, or put the final dot on your annual plan, step back and take a look at the ideas you have generated. If you're being completely honest, how many of those ideas do you believe your competitors have also come up with?

The honest answer we get when we ask our clients this question is anything from 80 to 100%. Shocking isn't it when we are relying on these ideas to deliver growth in a competitive environment? Most of us are wrapped up in a busy schedule and rarely question the quality and potential uniqueness of our ideas. We also fail to question the source of these ideas.

The truth is that competitive organisations are not always as competitive as they'd like to think they are. For a start, they often draw on a remarkably similar skill base, employing similar people from similar backgrounds. What's more, they have access to very similar data, and talk to similar consumers in similar ways. They get excited when they spot a 'new' insight in some data, but 9 times out of 10 competitors will be looking at the same information and getting excited about the very same insight!

You can see this in almost any category of product or service. Companies launching similar initiatives at similar times in similar ways. So much of what is expected to be step-change innovation is little more than another ride on the merry-go-round of incrementalism. There is a very simple law in operation here. If you like it's the first law of creativity – the quality and uniqueness of *stimulus in* has a direct impact on the quality and uniqueness of *ideas out*.

This is the basis of freshness, and it's why creative people and organisations do not rely solely on the same milk that their competitors are drinking. They source a wider diet, seeking out new experiences and ways of thinking about their market, products and internal processes. This provides the critical stimulus that allows them to see and think about issues in a different way. The new perspectives they gain provoke them into making creative connections that others won't have made. As Body Shop founder Anita Roddick puts it, 'Go where your competitors can't or won't'.

Stimulus is any experience that is new to you or outside the boundaries of the problem you are dealing with. This is important. Stimulus is not a new idea in itself but may be thought of as the raw material of the creative process. The stuff that's needed to do the job. Let's set things out clearly from the start and debunk some of the old myths about being creative. In our experience, if you've got good stimuli, you won't be able to help yourself from being creative – the unique connections will just flow from it.

Some people are highly disciplined about taking in fresh new experiences. They deliberately organise experiences for themselves and their teams and put structures in place to make sure they happen. For others the process is more intuitive.

Their raw material for creativity is constantly topped up by a deep, almost childlike curiosity about the world. Whether by design or instinct (or a bit of both) the most creative people and organisations ensure a very varied diet. Freshness can be both a personal and corporate behaviour. It is the behaviour that secures genuine competitive advantage, because true Freshness is impossible to replicate.

In summary, the behaviour of freshness is the continual search for new experiences that jolt you into making new and unique connections. Whilst creativity may appear entirely intuitive to the unaware, it is in fact a skill that we can develop, practise and plan into our everyday lives. This chapter will show you how. It will explore just why stimulus is so key to creativity and explain how you can inject freshness into your working life in both the long and short term. We will introduce the concept of 'river-jumping', using four techniques to stimulate fresh thinking at any time and then explore the long-term behaviour change necessary to build up your 'Freshness Store-cupboard'.

But first, we must take you on a brief journey to explore the workings of that most amazing human organ, the brain. We will show you why your brain is hard-wired to make creativity less easy and why you must use stimulus to trick the brain out of its non-creative channel.

'New ideas come from differences. They come from having different perspectives and juxtaposing different theories.'

Nicholas Negroponte

The world's greatest filing system

The human brain is an awesome piece of equipment. Unfortunately, it comes without a users' manual. Since the late 1950s a huge amount has been learnt about its structure and abilities, yet very few people have been taught how to maximise its potential. It has been discovered, for example, that the brain's main default setting actively inhibits the ability to think creatively.[1] Unless you learn how to work around this, your potential to produce new ideas will be severely inhibited.

The brain is what's known as a 'self-organising mechanism'. It automatically sorts all the data it takes in without us having to think consciously about it. Like a huge filing system, information is digested and stored in a logical and easily retrievable way.

The brain classifies and interprets new information by looking for similarities with what's already on file. So when you see something new, your brain will automatically ask 'what have I seen like this before?' It then opens that file and uses the memories stored there as a point of reference to generate thoughts and make decisions. You can see this in the exercise below.

[1] Dr Edward De Bono was influential in this area and introduced the term 'lateral thinking' into everyday use.

> **Try this**
> Faced with any situation, the brain's automatic response is to put us into a river of thinking based on previous experiences. If you want to test this, next time you go on a long car journey, try this simple game. When you pass a car and catch a glimpse of the driver and passengers, make up a story about who these people are, where they are going, and why. It's amazingly easy to do. From just a quick glance at the make of car, the ages and dress of the occupants and other details, a whole life can be imagined. This is the brain's filing system at work.

Human beings have the capacity to take in huge amounts of information. The sheer volume of data we absorb means that it would be virtually impossible for us to work out and interpret everything from first principles. Instead we use educated guesses based on similarities and past experience. The brain simply says, 'I don't really need to know, from first principles, how to act, respond or judge a certain situation every time I see it. What I'll do instead is direct you, based on what I've seen before that looks similar.'

So, people we've never met before are unwittingly classified by their looks, accent, clothes etc. – 'first impressions last'. Most of the time we take it for granted that the food in front of us is healthy and won't poison us. We assume that if we put our hand in that fire it will burn us, and so on.

If you imagine this process visually, information is like rain falling on a mountain. The brain decides which river to funnel the water down by looking for similarities

Have you ever watched a litter of piglets feeding?
They push and shove to get a teat of their own,
but you know they're all drinking from the same milk.

Most companies approach innovation in the same way.
Business is obsessed with 'best practice' not different practice.
Is it any wonder, then, that products, services –
and even companies – are increasingly hard to tell apart?

Creative Behaviour One

Freshness

with past experiences. The more these classifications get used, the deeper the rivers become. Imagine how paralysing life would be if the brain didn't act in this way. On average we put on seven or eight pieces of clothing each morning (socks, pants, shoes etc.). Imagine if we had to try each one out every time to find out where it fitted best! In fact, it has been calculated that there are over a million possible combinations for how we could wear these pieces of clothing. Fortunately, our brains don't bother us with all these possibilities. Instead the brain simply says, 'that looks like a sock, it'll go on your foot'.

This basic brain classification system has been developing and growing since we were born. An infant's brain is bombarded with millions of new pieces of information which fall like raindrops. The brain starts classifying, creating streams of recognition, which speeds up the sorting process, allowing it to handle more information.

The process continues at school. Over time, we get faster at classifying information by recognition and the streams become deeper. With good teachers, we continue to add new streams to the existing ones as new and stimulating ideas come along which challenge our preconceptions. Then we leave school or college. We start work. After the initial excitement of learning about this new environment, the flow of new ideas starts to slow down. But the flow of information speeds up. Our streams become rivers – and to handle more and more rain, the rivers get deeper.

As you can see, the brain's classification system has huge advantages. It allows human beings to handle vast amounts of data. But there are two big drawbacks to making such rapid classifications. First, the assumptions the brain makes can sometimes be wrong. This can cause us to jump to conclusions, to make snap decisions about people and situations, based on bogus assumptions.

Second, the way the brain processes information kills creativity. Every time we try to think of something new, the brain keeps bringing us back to the original river. Try to think of a radically different sort of car, for example, and the brain automatically reverts to the river of thoughts about cars. We soon find we are thinking in terms of a metal box with four wheels, even though this is not the only way of expressing a family mode of transport. The brain is leading us to a 'this is how it is' rather than a 'this is how it could be' scenario. In essence, every time we try to go off down a side stream of our river, the current forces us back into the present reality. We might stick a toe in the new stream, but we certainly won't be having any radically new ideas.

So how can we break this cycle? The answer is deliberately to find a way to override the brain's classification system. In short, we must trick the brain into believing we are thinking about another river. We must get out of the original river altogether, then re-approach it from a new and different perspective or river. This is what's known to most people as a lateral step – we call it river jumping.

Let's look at an example. Imagine we're trying to invent improvements to a photocopier. Say we start with an insight based on customer research. It tells us that a key issue for the end-user is that the traditional machines have an annoying habit of getting jammed, or blocked, at critical moments. The company that solves the problem will have a competitive advantage. What's needed is a flash of creativity. But because of the way the brain is wired, every time we try to think about new and different things to do with photocopiers, the brain will keep bringing us back to the river of current realities and past experiences it has already created. It will be virtually impossible to consider alternatives that challenge the classifications and rules that have been set up in the mind. We can develop and stretch the current parameters – maybe using a different roller to feed paper in will help, for example. But no matter how much we try to discover a tangential stream, the current of the original rules and assumptions will keep bringing us back. So we have to use techniques that enable the brain to make new connections. This is where river-jumping comes in. Using a piece of stimulus, we can focus on something completely different, breaking out of the photocopier river of thinking.

It goes something like this. The problem with photocopiers is that they can get blocked. First of all, and this is important, forget photocopiers altogether. Use a piece of stimulus to look at the issue from a fresh perspective. What else gets blocked? Noses get blocked when we have a cold. Think about noses. What happens now is that the mind instantly forgets all its rules and past experiences of photocopiers and starts reminding us of the things that relate to noses – which is a different river altogether.

We've made a lateral step. Now from this very different place turn round and make a connection back to the original topic. In other words, use the nose as a piece of stimulus to think differently about photocopiers. What happens when your nose is blocked? One of the great things about noses is that even when you have a cold both nostrils rarely get blocked at the same time. Now refer back to the original problem. What if photocopiers had a second feed system so that when they got blocked or ran out of toner you just flicked a switch and a second system kicked in? This would relieve the end-users' frustration when the machine jams at a bad moment. Now, thanks to the stimulus, we have an idea that's worth building on. Ideas rarely emerge fully formed, and often need to be built by several rounds of creative iteration – but more on this later.

Remember the stimulus doesn't give the answer; stimulus is not an idea itself, it simply provides fresh context and perspective. Stimulus allows us to jump out of one river of thinking into another – making a lateral jump. From this new river we can get insights to make new connections back to the first river. And guess what? Now it's much harder for someone else to follow, and to make the same connection. In fact, the more rivers we jump in the creative act, the harder it becomes to follow.

But be aware, the deeper the river of thinking – and let's face it, most of us are doing the jobs we're doing because we have deep rivers of expertise – the more difficult it is to jump out of our river or realise we're in one in the first place.

So what is this stimulus stuff? Stimulus can be anything that's not in our current river of thinking. It simply jolts us out of one river and into another. That jolt – or jump – is what allows the brain to create alternatives.

'Problems cannot be solved by thinking within the framework in which they were created.'
Albert Einstein

Greg Garrison's flight of fancy

In 1993, Greg Garrison was put in charge of a key initiative at the financial services and information giant, Reuters. Garrison was given the task of improving the usability of the computer trading systems the company supplies to the dealing rooms of banks in over 130 countries.

A key aim of new product development was to ensure that computer systems – especially the graphical interface that the customer sees – can be mastered quickly, so that dealers minimise their down time. In a business where $millions can be made and lost at the stroke of a keyboard, users of the Reuters systems were understandably reluctant to spend time retraining. Usability is vital. They said they didn't have time to read instruction manuals, but were adept at feeling their way.

What was needed, the Reuters team realised, was a graphical interface that was intuitive – easy to learn, and to master updated features. With the launch of the company's new product range approaching, the team sought inspiration. But in the pressure cooker atmosphere of the company's London base, the creative juices didn't seem to be flowing. Even the cool-headed Garrison was starting to worry. A breakthrough was needed. But it wasn't going to happen in the office.

Garrison set off on one of his frequent fact finding missions, travelling to the Far East to talk to customers in other markets. Away from the hustle and bustle of the Fleet Street office, he relaxed. His childlike curiosity returned. He began to search out fresh stimulus to jolt his thinking around the task.

On his return flight he asked to see the flight deck of the 747 he was travelling on. Surrounded by a wall of sophisticated instrumentation, he was amazed at how pilots could move from one aircraft to another in the same class with such ease – and without retraining. When he asked them, the pilots explained that instruments were arranged in a logical and consistent way across the 747 class, which made flying one aircraft much the same as any other.

Garrison made a new connection. What if the graphical interface on the next generation of Reuters systems was modelled on a pilot's cockpit? It would mean that switching from one system to an updated system would be relatively straightforward. Back in London, he reported his idea to the rest of the team. The idea took off.

Team members built on the original insight, adding a range of features that included autopilots and navigators, which would help the dealers find their way around the new system. Like a pilot's instrument panel, the idea was to place technical support and training at the customer's fingertips. At the touch of a button, traders would be able to move from the realtime market environment into onscreen simulations, calling up features such as autopilot tools to steer them through products – without having to call Reuters for support. In the event, the system was not implemented in full as it was superseded by adherence to the new Microsoft Office style desktop environment. Nevertheless, many of the tools the aviation metaphor gave rise to were included in the next generation of Reuters products, providing trading and operating support for end users.

All because Greg Garrison looked outside the environment of his problem and gave himself the stimulus to make a fresh connection – that's the essence of freshness.

Learning how to do river jumping

So how do you get started? What can you do now to get freshness into your thinking? It is often assumed that creativity is a spontaneous activity, but creative people in the know use tools and techniques to push their thinking. Far from being spontaneous, they plan creative sessions in advance.

As we have seen, understanding the brain's natural classification system is the first step to managing creativity. The ability to make new connections is limited only by the ability to jump out of one river of thinking and into another. The tool you can use to do this is stimulus. Think of it as an investment. You devote a short amount of time to not thinking specifically about the problem or issue, but investing in the stimulus that will subsequently enable you to make far more, and far richer, connections.

Hundreds of tools have been devised to help people stimulate different thinking. What they all have in common is that they are based on the principle of jolting the brain out of its current river of thinking. Most people struggle to remember more than three or four of these tools. You can quickly get bored by them – or realise that the techniques are not suitable for solving all types of problems. So, rather than provide a long list of tools, what we've done here is to try to pull back a bit and identify the principles that lie behind them. There are in fact only four main categories of behaviour that jolt your thinking. We believe at least 95% of all creativity tools fit into one of these areas. Once you understand the underlying principles, you will be able to invent your own techniques tailored to the exact challenge you are working on at the time.

Here we look at each of the four principles in turn and offer some practical examples of how they can be used. Don't worry too much about remembering all the detailed examples. If you understand the principles you'll be able to invent your own tailor-made tools to fit different situations.

To make them slightly easier to remember, each principle name starts with the letter R. We call them the 4Rs. They are:

Re-expression
finding an alternative way of describing or experiencing the issue or problem.

Related world
looking at other areas where a similar issue or benefit can be seen. This is the technique used in the photocopier example above.

Revolution
identifying and then challenging the rules and assumptions we are using.

Random links
making connections and links between the issue and random items found in the world.

Let's look at each of these in more detail.

First R: Re-expression

The way tasks and issues are expressed in business tends to be quite limited. Often we rely on business jargon and descriptors, which send us off down the same old rivers of thought. Simply describing or experiencing the issue in a different way will automatically prompt the mind to approach it from a fresh perspective, because the brain will put the new words into a different river.

You can get started with our favourite three re-expression tools.

1. Re-express with alternative words
As implied, simply replacing key words in your creative challenge will enable your brain to think in a different way. There are many words we use in our business lives which become loaded for us with a certain meaning. When we hear them, our brains automatically send us into a well-worn river of past association. Re-expression is a technique which tricks the brain out of this often non-creative assumption making. If you look at the loyalty example below, you can see how using many different expressions gives the brain lots of potentially new connection points back to the original problem. Similarly, we may re-express loyalty as a powerful metaphor, for example, 'like a marriage' – we could then think of the many different ways loyalty is encouraged in a marriage: courting, ceremony, public commitment, legality, pain of divorce – and use these fresh perspectives to help us reconnect to our 'loyalty' issue.

Loyalty

We recently worked with a major blue chip business to help it find more creative ways of increasing customers' loyalty. Having asked the obvious questions about what loyalty meant (increased purchase, greater share of purchase, etc.), we set about trying to re-express the challenge.

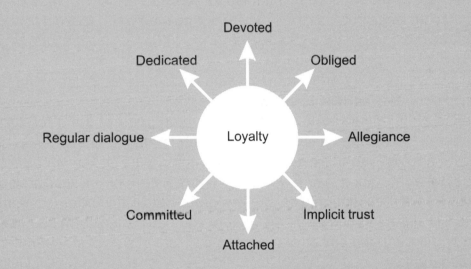

Simply by using alternative words we were able to expand the perception of the problem and open up new avenues of thinking. 'Allegiance' led to an idea about clubs which consumers paid to join while 'obliged' led to an idea about a penalty scheme for lack of loyalty.

2. Re-express using different senses

Using words is only one way to be creative. We have many other senses open to us which we use freely as children but hide away as adults and especially as business people.

For example, instead of relying on words, why not use a drawing to describe an issue, make a clay model or even act it out to make a physical representation of an issue or a business process. This may all sound a bit weird. We only suggest it because it works.

For example, we were asked to come up with new ideas for redesigning a busy street in the centre of London. Everybody in the creative session knew this street, and so instead of remaining in the world of words, we got them to stand up, choose a role – policeman, shopper, non-English speaking tourist, shopkeeper, taxi driver – and act out a typical scene from the centre of London. Shoppers bumping into each other led to an idea about arrows on the pavement directing shopper traffic flow. The commotion on the street outside the shops led to an idea about internal shopping walkways that meant you could pass from shop to shop without going back to the street, or overhead walkways or pedestrian-only zones …you get the idea.

'Originality is nothing but judicious imitation.'
Voltaire

3. Re-express from someone else's perspective

Try deliberately describing the world and your issue through the eyes of someone else. For instance, how would an alien describe this? How would your most feared competitor describe it? What about a five-year-old? The creative options are endless.

Liquid teeth

A client once gave us the challenge of launching a toothpaste in countries where the use of toothpaste was very low. The creative session had hit an all time low. The scientist attempting to explain how toothpaste works to the creative team assembled was having a hard time. His molecular structure diagrams were not helping us understand the benefit of the product. Through the glassy-eyed mist we suggested that he explain it to us as he would to a five-year-old.

'Well kids, teeth are made of calcium', he said, feeling rather embarrassed. 'And the amazing thing is that toothpaste has calcium in it too!' 'Wow', said one bright spark as a creative connection was made. 'Could we talk to the target market about liquid teeth?!'

Before long we were tumbling over ourselves to offer ideas based on a toothpaste tube full of liquid teeth – a great creative idea and all because we tried to re-express our challenge from someone else's perspective.

Second R: Related worlds

Never assume that you are the only person to have faced an issue like the one you are facing, or that you cannot learn something valuable from the world around you. 'Related worlds' is a technique that enables you to harness the experiences of others in a creative context. It is the art of identifying situations or events that in some way mirror the creative challenge that you face right now. You probably won't want to steal their ideas or experiences directly, but the principles or stimuli of another's approach can be identified and reapplied to your own challenge.

This is what management writer Tom Peters means when he refers to business people 'swiping with glee'. It is the very opposite of the 'not invented here' syndrome. It means deliberately encouraging people to go out and see what they can learn from others. The creative act occurs when you reapply this to your own challenge in a unique way. The roll-on deodorant is exactly this principle in action. The steal was to look at the ball point pen and apply the same principles to deodorant – another world where a liquid had to be spread thinly across a surface.

This behaviour is enshrined in the philosophy of Proctor and Gamble. The company has seven core competencies on which it focuses all its development and recruitment efforts. One of these is innovation and creativity. The guidelines on how to assess whether this behaviour is being exhibited expressly ask managers to look for evidence of employees 'seeking and reapplying'. The aim is to seek insights from related markets and reapply them closer to home.

Related worlds is a great principle for demystifying the creative process. All you have to do is ask 'where in the world has my challenge (or anything like it) been faced before? What can I learn and steal from that?'

To apply the technique start by considering, 'what am I trying to do, or achieve?' Write this as a short summary in the middle of a circle with a set of spokes coming from it. Now invest some time in thinking where else this issue has been encountered. Before long you will have a fabulous wheel of related world stimuli to base your creative thinking on.

Making music easier to buy – Virgin Music

As befits their continual focus on the customer, Virgin Music engaged us on a project to help make store layout easier to access for consumers who weren't necessarily music experts. (Virgin had learnt that non-music experts were finding it hard to find what they wanted in music stores.) We decided to do a related world exercise. It looked like this:

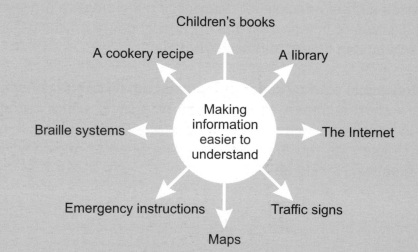

We then spent time investigating each of these worlds – drawing out principles and insights that we could reapply to our own issue. For example, when we looked at maps we realised that they cleverly used lots of symbols to convey complex information. From there we had the idea of creating a symbol for each different sort of music and posting a big visual key right at the front of the store. Use this example above to see what ideas it prompts for your local music store.

Related Worlds are everywhere. To start you off try the following.

Other businesses

When was the last time you visited a business outside your category? On a recent project about speed to market, for example, we sought stimulus from McDonald's (an inspiring speed system in action) and Formula 1 cars (pit stops reduced from 6 minutes to less than 15 seconds in the modern age). You can guarantee someone else somewhere has faced a challenge of a similar nature to the one you're working on right now.

Other people with related expertise

We call them 'naive experts' – people expert in your challenge area but not in your business. In a workshop we ran with a food company, our brief was to provide new ways of thinking about health. The brand team – stuck in busy day-to-day jobs – had no way of experiencing fresh perspectives. So over the course of a day we introduced them to eight different 'health experts'. These included the owner of an alternative practice clinic, a gardener, a super-fit 80-year-old, a slob (no interest in health), a personal trainer, a homeopath, a faith-healer and a doctor. Our challenge suddenly felt very new and very broad.

The wider world of science, history or nature

Did you know that Velcro™ was invented after a day of hunting in the Jura mountains in France in 1941 by George de Mestral? Carefully inspecting the burrs in his wool pants and his dog's coat, he found hundreds of little hooks engaging the loops in the material and fur. This natural hook and catch system gave him the initial idea for Velcro™. De Mestral went on to make a machine to duplicate hooks and loops out of nylon.

Third R: Revolution

Revolution is creativity at its most provocative. It's the deliberate challenging of the rules and assumptions that exist. Think about it, some of the great creative leaps of our time have come from Revolution. What if we could fly? What if we could have sex without babies? What if!

Very often our ability to come up with innovative ideas is limited by the rules that define our particular river. As we saw earlier in this chapter, the mind continually judges ideas and stimuli to try and make them fit with what we know already. Revolution is all about deliberately breaking the mind's rules. So the first step in revolutionary thinking is to be aware of the rules which already exist – in life or in your mind. This can be hard, so deep are the rivers we're in or so strong are the rules that exist. For instance, nearly all generations of writing implements have copied the original Quill shape: Ink Pen, Pencil, Biro™ and Roller Ball. It's only recently that pen manufacturers have started to change the rules with inventions like the ball shaped pen which actually suits the task of writing better.

When faced with a creative challenge, one of the simple techniques to get you started is to write down the rules. Question everything and get as many as you possibly can down on paper. What's the shape, usage, feel, touch, application, aesthetics, dimensions, process, etc. etc.? Below is an example from the world of shampoo.

Rules	Revolutions
It's liquid	Solid, a mousse, a milk, a cream, etc.
In plastic bottles	Capsules, a beautiful glass bottle, a fabric, etc.
For washing	Cleansing, massage, stimulation, cutting, etc.
Used with water	Dry with your hairdrier, a gas, etc.
Once a day	Morning and night, on the run, at the office, etc.
For beauty	Invigoration, repair, sensitising, pleasure, etc.

You can break each rule in many ways, each of which offers the chance of a fresh perspective or new idea. Once you've got your rules you can start to play around with them. For example, try exaggeration, opposing, reducing, and reversing as many of the assumptions as you can.

Five of our favourite revolutionary questions are:

1. What if we did nothing?
Rather than getting worried about the difficult-to-pour super-thick consistency of ketchup, Heinz simply turned this feature into a benefit. The advertising campaign leaves a clear message – if it comes out too easily then it must be low-quality ketchup.

2. What if we had to make it for half the cost?
The humble Mars Bar is a great example of revolution thinking. By filling the centre of chocolate with other lower cost sweet ingredients (toffee and caramel), the confectionery market was created and Mars had a worldwide best seller.

3. What if people bought twice as much?
What do you get if you double the size of a shopping basket? A basket you can't carry or a basket with wheels. The supermarket trolley was born!

4. What if we reversed the process?
Back at the end of the 1980s most car companies were concentrating on big, modern family cars. Two Japanese designers at Mazda reversed this thinking persuading the company to launch a retro racer based on the Lotus Elan. The MX5 (or Miata as it's known in the US) was launched and the two-seater sportscar market reborn.

5. What if we exaggerated the issue?
The potato chip was born out of the frustrations of a chef tired of complaints about the thickness of his fries. He decided to exaggerate their 'thinness' and made a famous discovery.

A handwriting revolution

The computer company 3Com's revolutionary Palm Computing Platform is a brilliant example of revolution thinking. In the new hand-held computer market one of the holy grails was a handwriting recognition system rather than a keyboard. Several technology companies had launched products (including Apple's Newton) but in all cases the handwriting systems were clumsy and inefficient. The rule which everyone had in their heads was: 'A handwriting technology which recognises everyone's handwriting.' This was the rule 3Com challenged. Their revolution was to create 'a handwriting alphabet which everyone can use'.

The rule breaking system 'GraffittI™' provided a set format of alphabet that the consumer had to learn. The revolution: train the consumer not the technology. As a result the technology required was much simpler and 3Com launched the Palm Computing Platform, on which all of its handheld organisers are based.

'Rules are for people who aren't willing to invent their own.'
Chuck Yeager, first man to break the sound barrier

Pollution solution

A few years ago, a city in the Netherlands had a refuse problem. A once clean section of town had become an eyesore because people had stopped using the trash cans. Cigarette butts, beer bottles, chocolate wrappers, newspapers, and other trash littered the streets.

Obviously, folk at the sanitation department were concerned, so they sought ways to clean up the city. One idea was to double the littering fine from 25 guilders to 50 guilders for each offence. They tried this, but it had little effect. Then somebody asked the following revolutionary question:

'What if, instead of punishing the people who drop litter, we reward those who keep the place clean?' At first this seemed daft – how can you reward people who put rubbish in bins?

Fortunately, the people who were listening to this idea didn't evaluate it in the context of current reality. Instead, they just asked in what circumstances it would be possible. In the end the sanitation department developed electronic trash cans that had a sensing unit on the top that would detect when a piece of refuse had been depositied. This activated a tape recorder that played a recording of a joke. As a result people went out of their way to put their trash in the trash cans, and the town became clean once again.

Fourth R: Random links

This is probably the principle that feels the most creative. It is the simple art of finding a person, object, place, picture or randomly selected piece of stimulus that has nothing to do with your creative challenge and then deliberately forcing a connection.

There are only two rules with this technique:

1. *The random item must be truly random.* You want items which have no connection with what you're working on. The random nature of the stimulus creates surprise and freshness.

2. *You must find a connection.* The harder you work to find a connection the more likely it is to be unique and therefore interesting. Remember what we said about competitive advantage.

For example, imagine you work in telecommunications. Can you force yourself into making a connection between a garden hose system (or lawn sprinkler) and a telephone?

Here goes: what if, like the sprinkler, the telephone had detachable equipment for listening or using, or you could attach equipment to the headset? Or the telephone was made for use outside so it's ideal for leisure clubs, outdoor occupations? Or what if, like the hose, you set up output points to connect telephone equipment into rather than investing in the hardware?

The point here is that the stimulus does not give you the idea. Instead it has a whole host of attributes, values and benefits which you can appropriate and adapt for your challenge. Its value is that it has absolutely nothing to do with your challenge so it will force you to think more broadly – in a way your mind without stimulus may never do.

Putting the 4 Rs together

An example brainstorm plan

The great thing about the 4 Rs is that they are not prescriptive. They are principles that can be tailored and adapted to any challenge. So when you're sitting at your desk with that 'empty head … where do I start' feeling, turn to the 4 Rs to get you started.

The 4 Rs can also be used in a much more formal way as the planning tool for a really good brainstorm session. Here is an example.

Our challenge was to invent breakthrough products for the hair care market. We gathered together a mixed team from sales and marketing, R&D, design and advertising agencies. We also invited some external participants, including consumers and a number of 'naive' experts from other disciplines to keep us fresh. Then for two days we immersed ourselves in a highly stimulated world based on the 4 Rs.

Used in this way, they can provide an incredibly powerful framework for creating brainstorms and ideas workshops. No more bare rooms, blank flip charts and blank faces. Instead, an inspired team constantly stimulated with fresh perspectives to provide the basis for genuinely new and different ideas.

	ACTIVITY	PURPOSE
Day 1 am	**Kick start** Facilitators welcome participants, play introductory games, set up the rules of creative behaviour, and explain logistics for the next two days.	Introduce participants. Create welcoming atmosphere. Highlight different way of working.
am	**Set up** Project leader sets up the challenge explaining what, why, parameters, purpose, etc. in a motivating way.	Participants have a common vision of what success is; they feel valued and motivated.
am	**First burst** Team gives opening thoughts and ideas they've already had for solving the issue.	People won't have new ideas until they've got their current ideas off their chests.
am	**Consumer workshop** Live consumer research 'focus' group using appropriate target consumers.	**Re-expression stimulus** Looks at the challenge from the consumer's point of view. Grounds whole session in consumer reality.

	ACTIVITY	**PURPOSE**
pm	**Act it out** Physically act out the whole hair care process from beginning to end as a piece of hair. (What does it feel like to be dirty/washed/dried/styled?) Experience acting out each new alternative.	**Re-expression exercise** Gets people out of their comfort/analytical zone to consider the feelings and emotions of the washing process.
pm	**Gym instructor/nutritionist** Half-hour talk on fitness and nutrition for the body.	**Related world exercise** Creates new concepts based around fitness and nutrition. It also gives us lots of new vocabulary concepts.
pm	**Hairdresser** Half-hour talk on latest styles and tricks and tools of the trade from a top hairdresser.	**Related world exercise** The professionals' view, very different from that of a major corporation, generated a myriad of new ideas
pm	**What if game** Series of provocative statements designed to challenge current world perspective e.g. 'What if products were twice the price?' 'What if you didn't need water?' 'What if shampoo didn't exist?' 'What if all products were solid?'	**Revolution exercise** Deliberate acts of provocation to focus people way outside the conventional market wisdom.

	ACTIVITY	PURPOSE
Day 2 am	**DIY** Participants washed their hair. One third washed as normal, one third with only one hand, one third blindfolded.	**Re-expression exercise** Stops people talking and makes them 'do' instead. Direct experience provokes new ideas.
am	**Beauty editor from *Cosmopolitan* magazine** Spends half an hour talking about the latest trends across the whole beauty market.	**Related world** A completely fresh perspective from beyond the world of hair care but from categories with real relevance.
am	**Foreign hair care reel** Ad agency collected together a 20 minute video of hair care ads from countries outside Europe.	**Re-expression/related world exercise** Moved us from verbal to highly visual interpretation of our challenge with very different cultural interpretations.
am	**Pottery class** A potter spent 30 minutes talking about the moulding and shaping of clay. He included tools and techniques used for styling and colouring effects.	**Related worlds exercise** Fantastically rich related world for styling products. The potter needs 'body and hold'.

	ACTIVITY	PURPOSE
pm	**Random box** Whole series of random objects taken out of a box. Participants asked to make connections.	**Random links** Freshness exercise designed to get us making connections and thinking outside the box of hair care.
pm	**Filtering and harvesting** Final two-hour session to give all the participants time to review the ideas generated.	Switching brain states from creative to more developmental/analytical.
pm	**Select leading ideas** Highlight areas for future development, pull out key learnings.	Giving everyone the chance to have their say.
pm	**Action/next steps** Focus on the key actions and next steps.	Maintain momentum and turn ideas into concrete business actions. Application of project planning disciplines.

Long-term freshness

So far we have concentrated on the day-to-day tools of creative thinking, the techniques that you can use straight away to radically improve the quality of your creative output. We know, however, from our own experience that this is only part of the picture. The skill of river jumping allows you to make creative connections in a particular moment, but a lifetime of continual freshness will give your brain a store-cupboard of stimulus, allowing you to make free-flowing connections at any time.

The freshness store-cupboard is your store of internal mind stimulus. It comes from your unique experiences of life, and you carry it with you always, using it to make connections whenever a creative challenge emerges. For us at ?What *If!* there are three types of ideas, as demonstrated in the model below. Ideas B and C can only come from planned stimulus, but idea type A can come at any time. And it is the quality of your own store-cupboard that dictates how good your free-flowing A type ideas will be.

Top of mind ideas. Sourced from your freshness store-cupboard	**A**	Automatic and intuitive
Ideas stimulated by river jumping techniques	**B**	Brainstormed and planned
Ideas built upon by team members	**C**	Co-operative and interactive

There is no hierarchy at play here. A good idea is a good idea no matter where it comes from (although you will often have to use all three levels to get a real breakthrough business idea). The behaviour of the freshness store-cupboard gives you the ability to operate quickly, intuitively and spontaneously. Let us explain.

Most people follow set routines at work and even at home. The concept of the freshness store-cupboard recognises this fact and deliberately does something about it. It involves going out of your way (and out of your comfort zone) to experience new things, meet people you wouldn't normally come into contact with and to see the world from different perspectives. It involves making a deliberate break with your usual pattern of life.

Breaking patterns is important because it provides a constant top-up of freshness. The freshness store-cupboard is kept well stocked by background stimulus.

This means that when you need to be creative, you have a ready supply of freshness to draw on to make new connections. This is the first place you access when trying to have new ideas in the absence of stimulus. So how do you do it? The tough part of pattern breaking is that it forces you to move outside your comfort zone. The reason most of us got into patterns or rivers in the first place was because they make it easier to cope with the demands placed on us. At work, this is about the demands of our jobs, but for many of us this spills over into our home

lives. At the weekend, we find we are more comfortable doing what we know than trying new things. Avoiding new situations becomes a coping strategy not just for work but for life. As we get older, and the demands on us multiply, most of us find we become more and more set in our ways. These patterns allow us to streamline our lives – avoiding situations and people we don't regard as essential to the tasks we have to complete.

Pattern-breaking turns this upside-down. It means making yourself do things you wouldn't normally do, or don't like doing. Faced with an invitation to meet new people or an opportunity to try something different, the logic of the accomplished pattern-breaker is: 'I'm not sure I'm going to enjoy this. Good, I'll do it anyway.'

In this way, the pattern-breaker ensures a diet of fresh experiences. At a simple level, going to new places provides more freshness. Reading a different newspaper or listening to a different radio station puts stimulus in the cupboard for a rainy day.

It sounds easy. But we've discovered the hard way that pattern-breaking behaviour involves some serious discomfort. It means reprioritising – and that inevitably involves some pain. But pain with a purpose.

'An idea is a feat of association.'
Robert Frost (1874–1963), American poet

Fresh today

Freshness is a difficult behaviour to acquire. By definition, it defies a formulaic approach. However with practise it's possible to make it part of your working life. Here are ten examples of practical things you can start right now!

1. Take a new form of transport to work next week. You'll be amazed at who you can meet and what you'll see.

2. Deliberately read a magazine or newspaper, listen to a radio station or watch a TV programme that you wouldn't normally see (children's TV is good for this).

3. Plan a monthly lunch with people from other parts of the business you don't usually consult. Chat to them about an issue they are working on and get their perspectives on issues you are working on.

4. Get out of your normal environment for at least half a day a week. At least 70% of what we think is the result of what's around us.

5. Ask your family (especially kids) to help solve a problem you're working on.

6. Allocate twice as much time as you normally would to solving a problem. Make sure you have at least three solutions before you choose one.

7. Block-out 'freshness time' for you and your team once a month. Go somewhere you wouldn't normally go together or do an activity you wouldn't normally do.

8. Take a walk in the park during office hours. Change the pace of your thinking. Take time to ponder.

9. Listen to the pop charts. (Do you know what's number one at the moment?)

10. Reinvent your job role at least once a year.

This represents the start of creating a freshness habit. Rather than relying on will power, create your own structures to make sure freshness is part of your life.

ICI

ICI paints division has the look and feel of traditional big business. We were invited in to start breaking a few patterns. Ian Kenyon had just been appointed head of innovation. He had a clearly defined vision and a realisation that if ICI stayed firmly fixed in the world of paint it would never hit the stretching business targets set by the wider company. But all around him and his team surged the fast-flowing river of paint. Paint products; paint business targets; paint market research. They needed some fresh stimulus.

As part of our creative journey together, Ian, team and ?What *If!* explored far beyond the world of paint. We set out to find some truly different related worlds. For example, we met a Colour Me Beautiful consultant who talked to us about how she matched colour to someone's skin tone and personality, then a colour psychologist who had a complex model matching personality types to tonal colour groups. (Interesting. Could we sell colour on personality types rather than simply names? London Retro Cool Colours range, for example, or English Country Lady range?)

A West End theatre lighting designer told us he could create any illusion with the use of light. (Interesting. Could we produce a range of paints that re-

---

sponded differently to different lighting conditions?) We met a fashion predictor – one of the people responsible for telling us that 'grey is the new black!' – while an interior decorator evangelised about how colour can change the mood. 'If I could paint the world', he said, 'I could change how everyone feels!'

Still more. An estate agent gave us tips for making a home more saleable. It's all about colour, smell, look, airflow (don't be fooled, this is a real art form). We talked to an Australian computer programmer who had created the world's first commercial 'room on a screen' interface, allowing DIY enthusiasts to experiment on screen rather than on their own walls.

The result of this work was a huge insight about how ICI wasn't really selling paint, but was in the mood creation business. This in itself opened up a number of exciting possibilities. One specific innovation was the creation of the world's first integrated home decorating solution. This system allows even the least accomplished decorator to integrate colours safely by sticking to a family of matching interiors which link colour on the walls to the décor around the walls. Consumers can create a whole range of room feels with different fabric, paints and furniture on screen before making a final choice.

A success story in the making? We hope so. But don't underestimate these two important points: it takes awareness to realise you're stuck in a river in the first place – this is the first key step that Ian and his team took. Second, a journey into the unknown comes at a price. More time out of the office; the uncertainty of success; the questioning of others from a traditional business world who just don't get it. Stocking the freshness store-cupboard is a real investment. And, yes, it is worth it.

Structure in some freshness

At the individual level, you can bring some freshness into your working life by becoming a pattern-breaker. We've come across a number of enlightened companies that have put structures in place to support this kind of behaviour (there are some examples below). Most companies don't. Does yours?

Superquinn

Fergal Quinn, the charismatic founder of the Superquinn supermarket chain in Ireland, wants his people to stay fresh and creative about food and ways of selling it. So he set up a system whereby everyone in the company (right down to the shelf stackers) is responsible for reading one food-related magazine a month. Each employee is allocated a specific publication from around the world to read. Their job is to use it as stimulus and send Fergal any ideas or observations.

Southwest Airlines

A few years ago Southwest introduced a scheme for people to spend one week every six months getting away from the office to have ideas about how the team was working and what they were focusing on. The scheme was so successful the practice is now encouraged across the whole of the business. Teams can go anywhere and do anything they like (within reason!) as long as they get stimulated to have ideas about how they can work most productively over the next six months.

Freshness Fridays at ?What *If!*

On the last Friday of every other month, the whole company stops work for the afternoon to join in a stimulus session. Responsibility for planning and organising is rotated so that everyone has a go. The guidelines are simple – the experience must involve the team doing something which we would never normally do and ideally feel a bit uncomfortable about. In these sessions we've: played bingo with pensioners in Camden, north London; drummed with African Dancers; had our fortunes told; got tattooed (removable after two weeks); been on the world's scariest theme park rides; visited Japanese supermarkets; taken part in Shamanic rituals; had Reiki sessions; run a children's Christmas party… and so on. Nobody tries to explain what we will get out of it directly – it's understood, it's our freshness store cupboard.

Ben & Jerry's Home-made

Ben & Jerry's Home-made Ice Cream is famous for its groovy flavours. Successes include Cherry Garcia, Chubby Hubby and Chunky Monkey. But coming up with new ideas year after year isn't easy. To stay fresh, the company has instituted 'Dessert Tours'. Folks from R&D Kitchen go on annual culinary tours of leading American restaurants on the East and West coast, chatting to top chefs and customers to get insights from the leading edge of food. They ask what flavours and ingredients are popular this season, and could be big in the ice cream world next. The only guideline is that they must eat as many desserts as they physically can.

Unilever

At Van den Bergh's, a subsidiary of Unilever, a sophisticated Freshness system has been designed. The 'germination process' as they call it, involves several people from every category team being nominated as stimulus hunters. Part of their role is to spend time out in the world searching for stimulus to jolt the rest of the team's thinking. Whole cupboards of stuff are collected and used throughout a project. The 'gemination process' is formal, structured, with clear responsibility lines and agreed budgets. It is a clear structural demonstration of the company's commitment to the principle of freshness.

Rover

In the UK, the car manufacturing company Rover introduced something called the 'REAL scheme' in the early 1990s to encourage staff to learn new skills. The company offered to contribute £100 towards any new learning experience outside of work that led to a qualification. Employees have gained additional qualifications in a variety of areas including foreign languages, SCUBA diving, football refereeing and massaging, all of which brought a wealth of freshness to people's thinking.

Richer Sounds

Julian Richer, founder of the hi-fi retail company Richer Sounds, has realised the benefits of getting employees out of the office. Each branch or department is expected to meet once a month. 'We don't pay for their time', says Richer, 'but we give them £5 a head allowance for liquid refreshment.'

His simple observation is that the primary thing employees have in common is their work. When they go out for a drink they eventually end up talking about their jobs. In the very different environment of the pub all sorts of fresh and innovative ideas start to emerge. Richer collects these using a simple ideas suggestion scheme.

Summary

The brain is not set up to make creativity easy. That's because the brain is hard-wired to use an automatic and subconscious classification system based on past experiences. When it takes in a new piece of information it simply classifies and interprets it according to what it has experienced or seen like it before.

This system is highly effective and allows human beings to process huge amounts of information very quickly. But it also keeps us locked into current and past realities.

To break out of this limiting mode of thinking, we have to distract the brain from its current rules using stimulus. By focusing on a piece of stimulus, we can then find a connection back to the original problem which allows us to see it in a fresh way (river jumping).

There are four basic river-jumping techniques:

Re-expression – finding an alternative way of describing or experiencing the issue.

Related worlds – finding an alternative but similar issue or benefit in another field.

Revolution – identifying then deliberately challenging the rules and assumptions.

Random links – using a deliberate connection with a random item.

Freshness

In the longer term, deeper freshness can be achieved by building up a personal 'freshness store-cupboard'. This occurs when we deliberately break out of the patterns in our lives and fill our minds with varied and unusual experiences.

And finally, remember freshness and stimulus won't give you the idea itself, they are simply the raw material for a new connection.

Creative Behaviour Two

Greenhousing

Plants are at their most fragile
when they are small and first starting to grow.
That's why gardeners use greenhouses.

It's the same with ideas —
they are easiest to kill when they first appear.

Unfortunately, most business cultures tend to
squash ideas before they can take root.

Is this you?

When you offer an idea, you are more often told why it won't work, rather than why it will.

You notice that not all ideas in the business are given a real chance to grow.

You are frequently so busy that you don't have time to discuss other people's bright ideas.

You hear yourself or others using phrases like 'yes, but …'; 'we've tried that before …'; or 'that won't work because …'

There are some people in your business you really don't enjoy sharing your ideas with.

'Greenhouse: light structure, mainly of glass used for rearing plants'.
Source: *Oxford English Dictionary*

'To Greenhouse (verb) to nurture fledgling ideas until they are big enough to look after themselves.'
Source: ?What *If!*

What is greenhousing?

A wise man was walking down a country lane when he happened upon a small genie sitting by the roadside. The genie smiled mischievously and confessed that as he had been discovered he must grant the man a wish. 'But to earn your wish', he said, 'you must first look at these two small shoots growing out of the ground and tell me which is the flower and which is the weed.'

The wise man paused, looked at the seedlings, and asked the genie if there were any rules to the challenge. 'Only that the answer is your own, with the help of no one,' replied the genie. With that, the wise man turned to leave and declared that he would see the genie again tomorrow. The next day he arrived with some compost and a watering can and tended to the seedlings.

Each day he returned and repeated his nurturing, until after a week he declared with total confidence: 'Genie, this is the flower, and this the weed.' And so it is with ideas. Just as it's not obvious if the seedlings will grow into weeds or flowers, so young ideas need time to grow and take root before you can judge their true worth.

Greenhousing is the behaviour that protects young ideas when they are at their most vulnerable, and nurtures them into healthy growth. It is an interactive behaviour that enables people to really get the most out of their initial thinking by supporting each other's ideas.

Greenhousing was born out of a realisation that creativity needs a different environment from that offered by normal business behaviour. It is an adopted, conscious behaviour that requires us to break some of our existing habits.

Normal business behaviour is characterised by rapid-fire decisions – the ability to analyse swiftly and make sound judgements based on the available evidence. It uses critical reasoning. Critical is a key word here. Analysis often involves an element of criticism. It's hard for young ideas to survive in this environment. If criticised or judged too soon, they wither and die. We have all experienced this. You offer a friend or colleague a new idea and you are greeted with the familiar response: 'Yes, but that wouldn't work because …'. The person making the judgement may indeed be correct. That is not the point here. The point is that by engaging their critical reasoning skills they have squashed the young idea. There is nowhere left for it to grow.

Greenhousing is different. The critical faculties are suspended for a period and the seedling idea given a chance to grow. All parties simply engage in nurturing ideas, making them as good as possible for a time. Greenhousing is fun, supportive and energising. It feels great, and it also requires some real discipline. You have to hold back those analytical thoughts and positively explore the new ideas. You are in the Greenhouse now, and you play by its rules. There will come a time when the ideas will be exposed again to sound business judgement, but that's not now, not yet – the ideas have to grow first.

The point to realise here is that ideas do not emerge fully formed. Creativity is rarely an 'apple falling on Newton's head' moment – a sudden flash of inspiration leading to the perfect invention. New ideas need to be developed in order to tell if they are indeed a flower or a weed. Greenhousing is the behaviour that facilitates this growth.

We believe Greenhousing to be at the heart of the creative revolution in business. In this chapter we: explain the principles behind greenhousing and in particular why we find it so difficult in our working lives; and provide a series of practical approaches to get greenhousing underway.

In the process you can look forward to the principle of looping the loop, getting more sunshine and less rain in your working life and discovering why an ancient Greek philosopher has a lot to answer for when it comes to killing ideas.

'A new idea is delicate. It can be killed by a sneer or a yawn; it can be stabbed to death by a joke or worried to death by a frown on the right person's brow.'

Charles Browder

Why greenhousing matters

Before exploring what you can practically do to bring greenhousing into your normal working life, let's take a moment to set it in context. If you look at the business environment right now, you can begin to understand why greenhousing is such a simple concept to grasp, yet requires real discipline to practise.

The last few years have brought massive changes to most businesses. The most significant trend is the move to fewer people doing more, with less time. This places a certain strain on us all. In response, business people have developed a set of skills and behaviours to help us cope.

Foremost among these is the ability to manage time and to make quick decisions. Our working lives have become a daily round of priority-setting; 'to do' lists; calls made; decisions taken; boxes ticked. We have become incredible task-performing human beings – or 'human-doings' as the latest buzzword puts it.

So frenetic has it become that today's business world often feels like an Emergency Room (ER) at a hospital – rapid-fire analysis of the situation, judgement, precise decision, prompt action. This is the way we work most of the time. Critical powers fully engaged. These are the positive aspects of ER behaviour. They are absolutely vital for the success of business and for the implementation of competitive innovation. But not on their own.

The problem is that the ER thinking style has become automatic to the point where it dominates in most company cultures. Often, it is the only approach that is recognised and rewarded within business. People are paid to deliver tasks on time and on budget. Organisations have a sense of the ER about them most of the time. But the ER environment on its own is hugely damaging to the growth of new ideas. If it is applied too early, it acts like poison on seedling ideas. ER behaviours have an essential role to play in the innovation process but must be kept out of the Greenhouse at all costs. This is incredibly hard to do.

The ER behaviours have become so ingrained, that for many of us they have become second nature, and we do not even realise that we are employing them – or, more precisely perhaps, that we have a choice of which behaviours to employ.

Try monitoring yourself over the next few days to observe what your first instinct is when you hear a new idea. For most businesspeople, it will be a knee-jerk reaction to judge. The first question that pops into most of our heads is 'Is this a good or bad idea?' This is usually closely followed by 'What's wrong with it? Are there any holes in the logic? Is it practical?'

These are the common thoughts that flit immediately onto the brain's radar screen. A classic symptom of this is the tendency to apply the ER interrogation to our own seedling ideas before they have been fully expressed. You can observe this in yourself and the people around you. How many times, for example, have you heard yourself, or others, start to describe an idea and then, even before the sentence is finished, explain the reasons why it wouldn't work?

To look for the root causes of this, we need to go back further than the modern business life of 'fewer people, doing more, with less time'. This has simply exacerbated a cultural norm that already existed. To find the birth of ER thinking we must go back much further.

Back to our ER roots

It all seems to have started in Ancient Greece, and in particular with Socrates, who initiated the Socratic tradition of logic and argument. The basis of this was very simple. Lacking the skills and tools to test the world around them scientifically, the great philosophers and thinkers of the age were left simply to theorise and guess about the nature of existence. Eventually a model or theory would be proposed and it was then the duty of all others to critique and challenge the version of reality which had been presented. If after serious challenge the theory still seemed to hold, it would be accepted as 'truth' until someone else could offer a better solution.

This style of thinking was rediscovered and taken to even greater extremes during the scientific revolution in the late middle ages. Suddenly, scientists had the techniques actually to test and prove a certain hypothesis. Critiquing, judging and challenging have been developed and fine-tuned ever since.

This logical, scientific thinking approach, relying as it does on the development of sharpened critical facilities, has now become the dominant thinking style employed in our modern education system. From the moment we go to school, we are trained in the discipline of logic; we are trained in the discipline of finding a right or wrong answer.

A recent American study, for example, calculated that by the time the average student reaches 18, he or she has completed over 2000 exams requiring a right or wrong answer. But in the initial stage of creativity, there is no right or wrong answer, there are only, and always, alternatives! Sadly, we have been trained – and are training the next generation – never to look for them.

The modern ER culture

It doesn't stop there. The ER culture is all around us. We are totally immersed in it from dawn to dusk. Turn on your radio and tune into a news or current affairs programme. Listen for the style of thinking that's employed. In most cases the aim of the interviewer is to find out what's wrong with what the other person just said. The line of questioning is designed to arrive at a predetermined journalistic position – to cause the maximum friction, and prove the interviewee wrong. Socrates would be proud.

The theory is that this confrontational questioning style uncovers the facts so that the members of the audience can make up their own minds. Once again, the main thrust is to have an opinion – to reach a judgement. But the proponents of this approach rarely take the time to explore the real meaning, the value, the goodwill or good idea behind the intention. Ideas are not fully explored. And then we sit and complain (judging again) that our political, cultural and sporting celebrities remain so tight-lipped with the media. They've learnt the harsh lessons of the ER world. It is not an environment that encourages people to open up and explore.

Politics provides the most dramatic example of the negative aspects of ER culture. So much of what we know of politics is little more than judgmental mud slinging – picking holes in arguments and in the people behind the arguments. Elections are won on 'negative campaigning' alone, often with little or nothing by way of positive ideas.

There has to be a better way. Imagine if we greenhoused our political, sporting and cultural figures even for just a short time. The level of creative debate would soar. Imagine a politician being interviewed in the Greenhouse, talking with scientists and other experts, to build ideas and make life better. Imagine hearing the politician say 'hey, I'd never thought of it like that before. That's a great idea we've developed here'. To do this, however, we have to let go of our ER instinct that demands an immediate judgement. Because of this, everything in the public domain has zero creative content. As a society, we force our most brilliant people to create behind closed doors, and then we complain about secrecy when they do.

If there are media people reading this book now, here's an idea that could give you a unique selling position. Call your slot 'The Greenhouse' and dedicate it to the growing of ideas. Set up a non-judgmental, supportive atmosphere. Invite celebrities to discuss their new ideas. Someone has to make a start.

The 10 best phrases to kill an idea

1. 'Yes, but ...'

2. 'We've tried it before ...'

3. 'That won't work because ...'

4. 'Have you really thought about the implications ...'

5. 'We don't have time for this right now ...'

6. 'Put it down on paper ...'

7. 'Haven't you got something better to do ...?'

8. 'What planet are you on ...?'

9. 'When you're in charge we'll do it your way, but until then ...'

10. 'That's fine in theory, but it doesn't work like that ...'

Why ER and the greenhouse don't mix

By now you can probably see the vital role greenhousing plays in the development of creative ideas and cultures. Injecting it into your business however is not easy. Most people start by trying to be more greenhouse-like in their day-to-day ER interaction. Unfortunately this can create more problems.

A real greenhouse is a total environment. Gardeners don't open the greenhouse door on a cold night to see what might happen. The results would be pretty obvious – damaged plants. The world of ER and greenhousing are two different worlds, and they mix like oil and water. They are characterised by different ways of thinking and behaving that completely cut across each other. To get the benefits of greenhousing requires adding a completely new and separate set of skills and behaviours alongside your existing ER ones. Both are vital, but only one can be used at any one time.

This is not a very well understood concept in modern business. Many businesspeople have quite simply never experienced a truly non-analytical, energised, building experience at work. Starved of this experience, they react to ideas the only way they know how – by judging them. This can lead to extreme frustration. The person judging the idea is often simply trying to help. The person having the idea (often unconsciously) begins to feel defensive. The result is a downward spiral.

Think of your own experience. In a meeting, you offer an idea that is then analysed by other people. The majority of the group may be in greenhouse mode, but it literally only takes one person to stay in analysis and the creative buzz is lost. As we noted earlier, the greenhouse is a total environment, it only takes one person to let in the antiseptic wind of the ER world and the seedling is lost.

The short-term effect of mixing these two worlds together is that ideas do not get properly developed. Remember, in business, ideas do not emerge fully formed. In the longer term, the effects are even more pernicious. People, bruised by the constant knocking of their ideas, stop offering the very seedling thoughts that are so crucial to success in today's competitive business environment. Creativity has suffered death by a thousand cuts. Little knocks that seem no more than throw-away remarks leave a lasting wound. The memory remains with the idea giver long after the interaction. There are the frustrated meetings; the managers you dread explaining your ideas to; that horrible humiliating defensive feeling you get inside when they point out just why they think it won't work. These experiences are still commonplace in our business community.

It is the long-term effect that is the most worrying. There are few things in life that are more personal than your own ideas. Reject an idea and you reject the person behind it. For some it can take years of reassurance to get these people to open up again and offer their creativity to the organisation.

Great efforts are now being made in the business community attempting to re-build creative confidence. That confidence has quite literally been analysed and judged out of the workforce by a business culture that does not understand the management skills involved in directing the human imagination.

It doesn't have to be this way. But to change it requires organisations and the people who work for them to master new skills and techniques. In short, to practise greenhousing behaviour.

Watching a film with a cynic – negative buzz

Ever watched a movie with a cynic? Someone who seems totally unable to suspend disbelief for long enough to enjoy what is intended to be an entertaining piece of make-believe. You have to put up with a constant stream of comments about how unbelievable the story is; how far-fetched the characters are; how completely implausible it is that they should behave that way. Irritating isn't it? That's what it feels like to share ideas with someone who is stuck in the ER environment. It's bad enough when it's a film or a book. But when the ideas are yours, you are bound to take their negative comments personally.

Living in the greenhouse

The rest of this chapter will focus on living in the greenhouse. Remember, when you're in there you must stick to the rules – with absolutely no exception. There is no middle ground.

So before we rush headlong into our new world it's advisable to check if that's where you want to be. For our 'greenhouse test' we use two quick checks.

First, what sort of behaviour is required? Do we need a decision, to share information, to judge a proposal or develop an idea? If it is the latter, go to the greenhouse. Otherwise, stay in the ER.

Second, where is the person I am talking to? If he or she is in the greenhouse, you will need to apply the behaviours in this section. If the person is still in ER and you want them to come with you to the greenhouse, you must *signal* your intent (covered in more detail in Chapter 5) so that they know the rules you're playing by.

At this point, you may be asking how much time you need to spend in the greenhouse. There's no fixed answer to this. For some business roles the balance will be tilted more towards greenhousing than for others. At the same time, there is always a trade-off between getting things done (ER) and nurturing ideas. It depends on your business, your role, and your vision for creativity within the organisation. But creativity won't just happen – you need to take responsibility and make the time.

The problem is that most people don't learn how to grow ideas. It isn't a behaviour that's taught in schools. We believe it should be. In time, as people become more aware of the role of creativity in business and every other sphere of life, we believe it will be. But until it becomes part of the curriculum, businesspeople will have to learn to teach themselves.

Some of history's worst ER blind spots

'I think there is a world market for maybe five computers.'
Thomas Watson JR – Head of IBM 1956–1970

'Who the hell wants to hear actors talk?'
Harry M Warner, Warner Brothers, 1927

'We don't like their sound. Groups of guitars are on their way out.'
Decca Records rejecting the Beatles, 1962

'(Television) won't be able to hold on to any market it captures in the first six months. People will soon get tired of staring at a plywood box every night.'
Daryl F Zanuck – Head of 20th Century Fox, 1946

'Everything that can be invented has been invented'
Charles H Duell, Commissioner of Patents, 1899

Being in the sun

The model we use to get people started is a simple one. In the natural world, the sun is the energy that drives all living things. Through photosynthesis in plants, it creates the basic fuel for life. The whole point of a greenhouse is that it lets in the Sun's energy and keeps out the rain and other harsh weather conditions that could damage the plants while they are at their most delicate.

You can think of greenhousing behaviour as creating an environment that lets in the sun and keeps out the rain.

SUN = Suspend + Understand + Nurture.
RAIN = React + Assume + INsist.

For the majority of us it's all too easy to let the RAIN into a creative situation.

When we first hear an idea, our instinct is to react quickly, to let our trusted analytical skills cut loose. We rarely take the time to check that we really know what the other person means. We assume that we know it, and immediately start to judge it.

Once it's started raining, both people tend to join in. Listening to your judgement of their idea, the idea giver gets defensive and starts to insist that the idea is right. You play your part by insisting back. The insisting passes backwards and forwards over the net like a tennis match. A highly charged match with the emotional strokes often getting harder, as each tries to smash the other person's argument and win the point. In SUN mode we suspend judgement. Neither participant is trying to score points. The tennis game becomes a deliberate attempt to keep the ball in play to understand and to nurture. What follows is an enjoyable and invigorating rally, where both players exercise their skill and wits in keeping the ball moving. Let's look at this model in detail.

Three stages of staying in the sun

1. Suspending judgement (Sun)

The first step of greenhousing is to suspend judgement. This requires the ability to consciously step away from forming an instant opinion. It's very difficult to do. You have to consciously disengage your mind from the normal ER response.

So when you hear an idea, stop. Pause … Now consciously choose to remove yourself from the ER environment. Don't worry whether it's a good or bad idea. It doesn't matter at this stage. The important thing is to suspend prejudice.

Let go of your critical faculty. Simply allow the thought to exist without evaluating it. Think of it as putting judgement in neutral for a while. Disengage action from possibility. Remember, you are not signing up to do anything except explore the idea. The reason you have to do this in a very conscious way is because you've been trained to judge.

Suspended judgement actually takes the pressure off you. You don't have to have an answer. You are like an open window – let the creative breeze blow through and ruffle your hair.

Put like that, it sounds appealing. But it's very hard to do. Nine times out of ten when we take an idea to a client we get a 'Yes, but…' response. You're probably judging what you're reading right now. Don't. Just go with it. Relax. Open your mind and explore the ideas here. You can decide whether there's anything in it later. Just leave the door open to the possibility. Live with it for a while.

We know how difficult it is to suspend judgement. We've been grappling with it for years. Our experience may be able to help you. Hard as it is, however, suspending judgement is not enough by itself. If you're not judging, what are you doing instead? You need to fill the space with something else.

This is where the other two elements of greenhousing come in – understanding and nurturing.

No zingers allowed

Some companies have developed their own structures to support the suspension of judgement. For example, in the US Southwest Airlines' 'University of People' is an official 'no zinger' zone. Zingers, in Southwest parlance, are 'undermining critical/judgemental comments'. So strongly does the university value its positive buzz that repeat offenders can be referred direct to the CEO to explain their negative behaviour to the company.

---

2. Understanding (sUn)

The second behaviour of greenhousing comes after you've made the conscious switch out of ER behaviour. You've suspended judgement, now you have to understand, and see the world through the other person's eyes.

Ask yourself whether you know what the hell they're talking about! You may have got the gist of it, but make a real effort to understand the idea – and the point of view that gave rise to it.

Now make the effort to let go of your own view of the world and see the issue through their eyes. Try to stand in their shoes. Understand how they see the idea, why they are motivated by it, what to them makes it good and why. Don't get too caught up in how the idea looks on paper – remember, there is no proven link between being creative and being articulate.

Understanding often simply involves empathy, using open questions to explore what lies behind the thought (what you've heard is probably the outcome of their thinking process). If you can tune into their mental wavelength, and really understand why they have said what they've said, then you are in a much better position to support it. Below is a simple set of questions to help you see the world through someone else's eyes:

1. Tell me more.

2. Why are you so excited about the idea?

3. How's it different to the way the world is now?

4. How did you get the idea/where did it come from?

5. What would it look like?

6. What do I stop doing in order to do what you're suggesting?

7. If I really believed in your idea how would I tell someone else the good things about it?

8. What would the consequences be?

Obviously, the greatest skill involved here is that of listening. It's hard work. Keep paraphrasing what you think they have said to check that you really understand it.

3. Nurturing (suN)

The effect of practising the first two behaviours of the SUN model is to create a supportive environment for people to share their ideas. However, this is not enough to produce ideas strong enough to leave the greenhouse. The final stage of the model, nurturing, is crucial to building stronger ideas.

Let's take a step back for a moment. We have talked about the fact that practical business ideas rarely come from a single flash of inspiration – they need to be built and developed. Without this vital final step, creativity can feel like a fun but ultimately wasteful activity.

We have come across many examples of businesses that through really good intentions have created a positive environment for ideas to come forward. Often this takes place in the protected environment of a brainstorm or creative session. Free from the fear of judgement – the ideas come pouring out. However, at the end of the session, what remains is a huge list of disconnected thoughts that rarely get followed up.

You can think of this as the difference between bungalows (single storey buildings) and skyscrapers. A bungalow is a thought or idea that doesn't get built on. A skyscraper is an idea that is built up through many levels to achieve its full potential. Competitive innovation is about building skyscrapers – the first level of an idea is not enough, we need to build further. So now it's time to grow green fingers. Practically we identify three key elements to the nurturing behaviour.

(a) Make it better or 'build it'. Don't just understand it, set out to grow it. Let's take an example. Say you work for an ice cream company and you're out to dinner with some friends. One tells you that she thinks that an after-dinner ice cream would be a terrific new idea. Your first response (your habitual ER reaction) is to think: *'Oh no, I'm not at work now. This isn't a new idea anyway.'* But you catch yourself, suspend your judgement and ask some questions.

'What made you think of that, Laura?' The chocolates are being passed round, and Laura confesses that she would like something a little cooler. The idea came from a box of chocolates. So now build on the idea – the ice cream could come in a box like sweets, with different centres; or using Belgian chocolate. Can you feel the skyscraper getting higher? (You don't have to make any decision yet, you're just relaxing to see where it goes).

(b) Seek value/find an angle. If you can't think of a building block that takes the idea on to the next level, simply try to see if there's anything in the idea that you do like. Look for a principle, or a concept behind it. Set out to discover if there is any component part of the idea that has value.

Let's take the ice cream example again. You've got to a skyscraper that has the ice cream packaged like sweets, with different centres and different types of chocolate. What is it about this idea that's interesting? Well, sweets are portable and convenient, and kids like them for their variety. OK, so maybe we've got an idea here for mini ice creams packaged like sweets. You remember a small piece of market research last year where mums were complaining about your ice cream getting everywhere – on the kids' faces, clothes, push-chairs (strollers). Maybe you have an idea here worth progressing. This is SUN in action.

The transistor radio

Ever heard how good the Japanese are at adapting technology? That's because they're great at seeing the idea within the idea. While it was the British who invented the transistor it was the Japanese who saw that the idea within the idea was small electronics for mainstream consumers. Based on this insight, the transistor radio was born – one of the founding blocks of Japan's electronic revolution.

Here your objective is to constantly look for ideas within the idea. Too often people only take ideas at face value. They are blinded by what they first see, so be a detective and look for what's within it.

(c) Find alternatives. The final nurturing behaviour is to keep pushing yourself to find another way. Now this behaviour really does go against the grain for most businesspeople. Trained as we are in the 'tick-box' mentality of getting things done as fast as we can, it's a real discipline to stay with an idea to generate fresh alternatives. But think for a second. It's a gear-shift most individuals and businesses don't have. We see this most obviously in the creative challenge sessions we run. For

the majority of creative tasks we run 90 to 95% of the teams answer the challenge in the same obvious ways. It's the same in business. The need to do *now* dominates the need to do *smart*. The habit of forcing yourself to explore alternatives can very quickly change this.

Take our ice cream example for the final time. We started off with chocolate box ice cream and mini ice cream sweets for kids but surely there are other solutions. Don't stop now you're on a roll. Chocolate box ice creams could also be re-expressed as ice cream gifts. Where does this take you? What about ice cream rock with the name of your recipient inside? What about sculptured ice cream cake as an impressive after dinner desert, or what about an ice cream game you could play after dinner and eat? Each has the potential to be a new source of ideas ready for more greenhousing.

Nurturing is an underrated and powerful creative behaviour. It relies on three things: building, seeking value and finding alternatives. What follows is a great example of all this in action.

Snapshots

The following is a real example of greenhousing that led to the launch in 1999 of Snapshots – the world's first flavoured carbonated spirit sold in a shot glass. This is a recollection of two or three minutes of a stimulus and ideas clinic we ran with the senior marketing and development team at Bass Brewing in the UK. It was one of those times when the energy just seemed to flow.

We blindfolded the team and gave them a series of weird and wonderful taste experiences – from cold baked beans to chilli peppers to chocolate.

The idea was to get them to think about alternatives to the traditional drinks experience. One specific stimulus was an ice cube made from pure lemon juice.

The instant it exploded on the taste buds, people were shocked, spitting it out, shouting and generally questioning what sort of sadistic maniac had convinced them to do this. But, at the same time, we managed to suspend judgement. This allowed the group to start exploring what could be. The conversation went like this:

Conversation	Commentary
'Yeuch. I'd never drink that in a month of Sundays.'	Initial strong reaction
'OK, OK, but what principle could you steal from this to create a new drink?'	Suspend judgement and explore
'Well, it's certainly a shock to the system'.	State principle
Yeah, it goes straight to the back of your head.'	Understand and explore
'I like that – a drink that goes straight to the back of your head. Feels like a big head rush.'	Nurture and build

'Like champagne with sugar and brandy; the bubbles go straight to your head.'	Explore
'So what if you could put pure bubbles in someone's mouth?'	Nurture
'Then down them in one, like a Tequila shot.'	Build
'You'd sell it in a shot glass. You know like the girls in the Mexican bars.'	Understand and explore.
'So what we've got is a champagne slammer sold in a shot glass.'	Build
'Yeah, only it could be vodka. It's much cooler.'	Build
'And you'd probably flavour it as well.'	Build

This is what you want more of! What's brilliant is that by the end of the session it's no longer just one person's idea, it's the team's idea. This is 'ideas democracy' in action.

The result of this two minutes of greenhousing was a flavoured vodka drink sold in a shot glass. It was launched nine months later.

SUNdays at work

Our mission at ?What *If!* is to help business people realise that there are two worlds within business – the ER and the greenhouse. Each has different behaviour and thinking styles. With awareness, you can consciously switch from one world to the other at the appropriate time. This ability to make a mental and subsequently behavioural switch is covered in detail when we talk about the art of signalling in Chapter 5.

The benefits of the greenhouse are both personal and cultural. At a personal level, greenhousing behaviour is playful, youthful and full of the energy of growth. It is a fair place, offering protection from the sometimes harsh, judgmental climate outside. This is the palpable sense of excitement and energy we call the 'positive buzz' of creation. It's a hard thing to describe, but you know when you've got it.

Creative sessions without positive buzz can have a staccato feel to them. One person offers an idea and then someone else offers another idea, but there is no real connection between them. However, the snapshots example illustrates 'positive buzz', a time when ideas flow around a room, with each participant contributing without judgement, and each contribution improving and adding to the previous thought until it's time to move on to the next.

A sure sign of positive buzz is when you get to the end of a creative session and it's quite impossible – and irrelevant – to distinguish whose ideas were whose. At a personal level, this is the infective and joyful experience of creation.

At a cultural organisational level, greenhousing behaviour builds creative capacity and confidence over a period of time. It creates a ripple effect like a Mexican wave flowing through a sports stadium. If ideas are not subjected to a crazy notional pecking order, you will be amazed at the brilliance of those you work with. 'It's always the quiet ones', as the saying goes.

Greenhousing is an inclusive behaviour, involving all. A greenhousing culture, then, truly supports the release of an organisation's creative potential.

A ridiculous idea

In the early 1990s, a police task force was set up to tackle the rising tide of burglaries and theft in the UK.

In a moment of inspired lateral thinking, the revolutionary thought was that criminals be persuaded to identify themselves. The idea was radical – crazy even – but rather than crush it, the idea was built on.

How could the police get criminals to turn themselves in? What would tempt them to incriminate themselves? Further discussions led to the brainwave of placing wanted advertisements in local newspapers, offering cash for a quantity of televisions, video players and other household items popular with burglars and petty criminals.

The ads attracted truckloads of the missing equipment – driven by the very people the police wanted to catch up with. The sting was a great success, not just because someone had the wild idea that criminals could be persuaded to turn themselves in, but because the initial idea wasn't laughed out of existence – it was nurtured.

Sun and rain recap

	🙂	🙁	
S	**Suspend** The two-minute pause – every time you hear an idea you practice this drill. Visualise yourself sitting on their side of the fence. Give out positive energy	**React** React quickly with a view of your own. Remain in opposition; your focus is on your own arguments. Just do the above, and the negative energy will take care of itself.	**R**
U	**Understand** Really try to get inside the other person's head. Open questions: Tell me more… Let me understand… What else do you like about your idea…? Great listening. Paraphrase what you think they mean, and check you've got it right 'so are you saying that…'	**Assume** Keep thinking about your own agenda. Assume you know: I think… I know that… I only meant… Listen in order to pick holes in their argument/idea.	**A**
N	**Nurture** Make it better by 'building': 'So if you think X, maybe we could do X and Y'. Seek value/find an angle 'what's the big idea behind this idea'. Find alternatives: 'How else could we do this?'	**Insist** Find fault or 'knock': 'That will never work' . Find another flaw in the idea and insist you're right.'I know that won't work, we've tried it before'. Insist that there is only one way to do it.	**IN**

Knowing when to put up your greenhouse

So now you've got a clear view of the what, why and how, but you don't have the when. Greenhousing isn't a special performance behaviour. We want you to use it everyday. In this section we touch on two key moments when greenhousing is obvious, and when it isn't.

The fixed greenhouse

Most people will have experienced a greenhouse environment in a formal setting. A planned brainstorming session, for example, is a formal greenhouse with its own set of rules. Be positive, build ideas, have fun, etc. It's a big greenhouse with plenty of room for many people inside.

Other examples of this include fixed agenda items in meetings. The group sets aside a part of the agenda to generate ideas on a particular subject. Some companies have taken this principle a little further than most with specific number of days every month for individual creative time.

Similarly, some businesses have specially designated physical environments that they devote entirely to greenhouse behaviour. In 1998 Heinz converted a cottage in its grounds into a creative play space, complete with the material and the behaviours appropriate to greenhousing.

These formal greenhouse spaces – whether they exist in a physical sense or simply in the minds of participants – provide a very clear framework in which people can let their creative hair down. But greenhousing doesn't have to be restricted to a formal setting. You can also put a temporary greenhouse over a conversation that lasts just a few minutes in an ordinary working day.

The pocket greenhouse

There is another sort of greenhousing that is much harder to practice. This involves informal sessions that occur during the normal working day. Often they are just between two people. The knack to informal greenhousing lies in recognising a creative situation and putting up a pocket greenhouse on the spot. It may last just a few minutes, but it is a safe haven for creativity. Inside the pocket greenhouse, creative rules apply.

Accomplished greenhousers can switch out of an ER environment and change their behaviour to go into a pocket greenhouse when required. They recognise that it's part of their responsibility to support the creative culture.

But it is not easy. Sometimes it means seeking value in an idea that seems quite ridiculous at first. It requires a basic sense of respect for the other person. What you are greenhousing in these situations is the creative potential of the person, not necessarily the immediate ideas. The alternative is that you react in a judgmental way and squash the idea – and probably its originator, too. We recently came up with the crazy idea of Thompson Holidays hiring a US Marshall from the days of the Wild West. Like Clint Eastwood he would dispense justice in holiday resorts – sorting out holidaymakers' troubles with speed! At first we laughed at the idea but then resolved to stay with it – to nurture it. The result? Thompsons have now launched 'trouble shooters'. It's a unique service to deliver customer satisfaction on the spot and on time.

Think in terms of a mini-greenhouse that you carry around in your pocket at all times. It can be brought out and placed over a creative interaction at any moment. The essential component is awareness. Creative people recognise when greenhousing is appropriate and make a conscious choice to switch behaviours.

Once you become aware that a different sort of behaviour is required to support creative interactions, you are half way towards achieving it. The art of greenhousing is to identify when you are involved in a creative interaction and make the switch from the analytical mindset to the nurturing mindset. Once you recognise that your job involves two worlds instead of just one, this makes perfect sense.

Red card/yellow card

At the brewing company Bass, a traditionally robust male culture where sarcasm is a cultural norm, nurturing behaviour is supported by language borrowed from sport. When we explained our greenhousing phrase book (see below), we were told that the traditional Bass culture was resistant to what the company's managers called 'London Agency Speak'. Instead, they adopted a football analogy for individuals who trample on ideas.

During a football match, players who commit a foul are shown different colour cards by the referee to indicate the seriousness of the offence. Bass adopted a similar language. A simple warning is a yellow card (equivalent to a booking). A second offence or a particularly negative comment gets a red card (equivalent to being sent off) and the offender has to leave the meeting. It's done very playfully, but there is a really serious intent behind it.

The greenhouse phrase book

One of the key structures to support a shift in culture is to change language. In politics, for example, it can signal a break from the past. In the UK the renaming of the Labour Party to 'New Labour' was a great example of this. As Labour, or as it became known, 'Old Labour', the immediate associations were mainly negative (failed policies, poor presentation, weak leadership, infighting, etc). By deliberately shifting the emphasis to New Labour the party signalled a big shift and highlighted the change. No longer was the immediate reaction negative. Tony Blair and his team had the chance to create a new set of associations and feelings.

The same technique can be used very powerfully with greenhousing. Rather than waiting for language to shift, make it happen. Create a phrase book of the new language you want to hear. Be explicit, don't leave it to chance. By driving the language into the culture you'll be amazed at how quickly the shift to greenhousing begins to take effect. What follows are our favourites phrases:

Words or phrase	Why it's useful
'Brilliant…' 'Great angle…' 'I love it…' 'Excellent…' 'Wicked…'	Encourages and rewards people for their efforts. Promotes goodwill and extends energy. Generally done far too little at work.

Words or phrase	Why it's useful
'Let's try it out…' 'We'll go with this one for a while…' 'I'm not going to judge…' 'I'm not sure where this is leading, but so what…' 'No yes buts…'	Phrases which facilitate the suspension of judgement. Circuit breakers designed to tune us in to the new idea.
'How can we make this better…?' 'My build on your idea is…' 'Let's push this further…'	Forces people to make ideas better. Prevents them from slipping into judgement.
'What's the big idea behind this…?' 'What I like in the idea is…' 'The principle that I like is…'	Too often people see only the idea in front of them. These phrases force people to look deeper for value in an idea be it for a principle, concept or part of the idea they can use.

Words or phrase	Why it's useful
'Let's stay with this idea longer …' 'There's something great here, let's work on it…'	Focuses people on nurturing ideas rather than judgement. Encourages tenacity.
'So what's the big idea for you?' 'Why do you love it?' 'Where will it be most valuable?' 'How do you see it working?' 'Why is it better than what we're currently doing?' 'How would you develop this?'	Phrases that promote further exploration of the idea.

A lifelong challenge

Armed with the awareness of the principles outlined in this chapter, and with the presence of a little goodwill, we have seen organisations and the individuals within them significantly increase the creative buzz of their working lives.

There is no rocket science here. We believe that anyone with an open mind, and working in a supportive environment where the principles of greenhousing are understood, will be able to work successfully in SUN. Once you have become aware of your in-built behaviour of judging or analysing, it is not too difficult to catch yourself and allow a creative exchange to grow. However, for those who really want to develop their creative skills and get all they possibly can from this book, it is possible to push greenhousing even further.

So far we have talked about greenhousing in relatively easy conditions. Someone offers an idea and you respond in the SUN. They pick up on your positivity and respond back with more SUN behaviours. As we suggested earlier, this type of interaction is much easier in a 'fixed Greenhouse' (like a brainstorm session) where the environment is predictable.

However, we also talked about the principle of pocket greenhouses – business people with the skills and awareness to erect a mini-greenhouse over a certain situation, or business interaction. This obviously requires a far greater degree of skill because in this situation the weather is changing all around. That's just what business life is like – constantly changing weather conditions. In real life, and in real business, it is likely to RAIN at any time.

Metaphorically, it RAINs in our heads many times a day, and when it happens we find it much harder to practise greenhouse behaviours. So our challenge to create involves seeking to reduce day-by-day, year-by-year, the occasions when it rains, because this is what will stop us expanding creative potential. We call this expanding our 'ideas bandwidth'.

Lets face it, everyone has a view of how the world should be. This is shaped by opinions, values, self esteem, existing ideas and a view on how they and others should behave. Think of this as a bandwidth in the mind. When we hear an idea that fits inside our existing bandwidth, we find it much easier to respond openly. In these circumstances, it is much easier to operate with SUN behaviours and to create.

It's when we hear an idea or opinion, see a behaviour, or meet a person who doesn't fit our expectation that the real challenge occurs. Our natural defensiveness (fight or flight) is triggered by these events and ideas outside our creative bandwidth. When this happens, we react; we start being defensive. It starts to RAIN. From this position it's incredibly hard to create anything new, because the focus of our energy is spent defending our existing position.

The challenge for those who wish to truly excel in the practice of creative behaviour is to react in this way less and less. This requires us to literally turn the RAIN off in our heads when we feel the first few drops begin to fall.

To do this it's essential to recognise the (early) symptoms of RAIN. It produces a number of common reactions. If you feel any of the sensations below, it's often an early warning signal that it is about to RAIN:

1. Losing your temper

2. Feeling frustrated

3. Insecurity about the situation

4. Insecurity about yourself

5. Lack of respect for the person you're dealing with

6. Strong sense you're right (because you're an expert)

7. Reaction to criticism

8. Leaping to judgement

9. Justifying your idea

10. Rushing to tell the person they're wrong.

So what do you do in these circumstances? First pause (count to three), give yourself a few seconds to take stock and switch from RAIN to SUN. The act of pausing then switching is critical to avoiding automatic RAIN behaviour. It's hard, but with practice it can become an automatic choice.

Remember, moving into SUN mode doesn't necessarily mean you agree with someone else's idea. You can spend time in the SUN and then switch back into the ER world to assess what you've created. What it does mean is that you're always willing to make a choice to explore.

It probably won't come as a surprise to you that those people who find it hardest to remain in the SUN state – to remain open to creative possibility – are those who have a very narrow or fixed view of the world, which they hold onto at all costs. Because they have a narrow personal bandwidth, it is frequently being challenged as life happens around them.

It is even more difficult to remain in SUN state when you do not fully respect the people working around you. Lack of respect for others is the most fundamental barrier to SUN behaviour and creative potential.

From our own work in this area, we are well aware of just how difficult it is to stay open and in the SUN. But the benefits are truly enormous for those who have the personal bravery and strength of character to not get drawn into their own instinctive RAIN behaviour patterns. It allows you to open up your own and others' full creative potential – to engage with those around you and take the full value from those interactions. Over time, it enables you and others to expand your collective ideas bandwidth beyond its existing limits.

If you are inspired by this challenge, start taking notice of when the rain begins in you. Stop and make a choice to spend some time in the sun/greenhouse.

The key is to recognise that an idea is simply a stepping off point. It provides a seed for creative growth. The more an idea challenges your thinking, the more the potential to grow it into something that has never been seen before. Grasping this point, and not feeling threatened by ideas, boosts personal creativity. SUN behaviour nourishes all ideas.

'An idea is a point of departure and no more. As soon as you elaborate it, it becomes transformed by thought.'
Pablo Picasso (1881–1973)

Summary

Young ideas are easy to kill especially in the over dominant ER world of business.

There is another approach, the complementary skills set of nurturing and growing ideas – greenhousing.

Business cultures often do not reward, and frequently do not even recognise, the existence of this alternative way. As a result, ideas remain underdeveloped and people hold back their creativity – saving it for the weekends.

Our vision of the future is to encourage businesspeople to switch between the ER and the greenhouse at the appropriate creative moment. This means being in the SUN and staying out the RAIN.

Sun	Rain
Suspended judgement	React
Understand	Assume
Nurture	Insist

Greenhousing is not halfway behaviour; you must be right in the greenhouse with the door closed.

The obvious greenhousing structure is a brainstorm. However, it can be applied to any conversation. Be ready to put up your pocket greenhouse. Also use language to shift your culture into greenhousing, create a phrasebook.

Long-term, work on your ideas bandwidth. Learn to catch those moments of automatic RAIN behaviours more often. Make a choice to explore and expand your bandwidth.

Creative Behaviour Three

Realness

Why don't people get excited about ideas at work?
Even when you think you're really onto something,
they just don't seem passionate.
No matter how well you think you explained,
they just don't 'get it'.

Is this you?

You talk a lot about your plans before you attempt to make them 'real'.

Your meetings are filled with presentation slides, bullet points, spreadsheets, words, numbers and more words.

You and your people are distant from the world in which consumers make decisions.

Your interests and skills outside of work are rarely used in your professional life.

You rarely go home at night and show your family or friends what you've been working on and say 'Hey, look what I did today!'

'Real: actually existing as a thing or occurring in fact'
Source: *Oxford English Dictionary*

'Realness: bringing ideas to life in whatever way you can.'
Source: ?What *If!*

Get real

Realness is a simple but powerful concept. It demands that we stop talking or writing about innovation and ask: 'How can we make it real right now?' Realness is all about getting as close to a real experience as you can. It doesn't matter whether you are selling a product or a service, or if your market is a few people or a few million people, realness will give you new insights.

It's fun and it's fast and for most of us it involves a real revolution in the way we work. But rather than talk about realness – let's get real with some examples!

Credit card realness

Recently, we were presenting an idea for a radically new sort of credit card to a group of managers from a financial services company, which included the divisional director. Our basic idea was that all sorts of benefits and information could be offered on one single card. It would do more than just offer credit. Health insurance, vehicle recovery and a variety of other services would also be included.

Our client was sceptical. Could these disparate benefits fit together under one single card and concept? We attempted to explain why we believed consumers would readily accept the idea, but the client just wasn't convinced.

Then we produced a prototype – a fully mocked up version of the new credit card, complete with magnetic strip and an embossed account number. The whole tone of the meeting changed. Suddenly, the director became animated – passionate. He was holding the answer in his hand. He 'got it', and his colleagues got it, too. For the rest of the meeting, he kept picking up the prototype, touching it, and looking at it. For him, the idea had become real.

Tiger realness

In 1998, Disney opened its new $1 billion theme park, Animal Kingdom, in Orlando, Florida. Five times bigger than the original Disneyland in California, Animal Kingdom represents the most important addition to the Florida Disneyworld location since the opening of the Disney/MGM Studios in 1989. But the new theme park nearly didn't get built at all. CEO Michael Eisner liked the idea, but the strategic planners around him weren't convinced. They could only imagine a variation on the traditional zoo. To make matters worse, it coincided with the recession of the early 1990s and the theme park business was suffering. The champions of the new park, the famous Walt Disney Imagineers, were undeterred. This eclectic bunch of designers, artists, writers and engineers has been recreating the Disney magic ever since Walt himself sketched out the original plan for Disney Land. Heading up the design team was Imagineer Joe Rohde. It was his job to convince the planners that Animal Kingdom would be a radical improvement on the traditional zoo. He spent months trying to win approval for the new theme park.

But meeting after meeting failed to persuade the doubters. Finally, when Eisner wondered out loud whether the mere sight of live animals would be sufficient to excite visitors, Rohde decided it was time to introduce some realness into what was fast becoming a theoretical debate. At the next meeting, he brought with him a live 400-pound Bengal tiger. When presented with the awesomeness of the real experience, any intellectual debate about whether animals are or aren't exciting soon evaporated. Animal Kingdom got the green light.

Ref: Gunther, Marc, & McGowan, Joe, 'Disney's Call of the Wild', *Fortune*, 13 April 1998.

What holds realness back?

Realness is the art of bringing an idea to life in whatever way you can rather than relying solely on words and memos. The Disney tiger and the credit card story are exceptional in business. We find that most organisations have little awareness of the benefits and practice of realness. Instead, they have unwittingly created cultures where the medium of communication is primarily the written or spoken word.

There is nothing inherently wrong with words. Words are wonderful tools used in the right way and at the right time. The accuracy and efficiency of communication needed in the emergency room environment suits bullet points, memos and emails. But when it comes to creativity, 'word-only cultures' act as a barrier to innovation. Once you've decided to go into the greenhouse and into the SUN, words alone just aren't enough.

We have a saying at ?What *If!*: 'If you are not selling words then don't invent with them!' Like us, you've probably been in too many meetings with too many debates, producing too much hot air about a new product or service.

Consumers (customers, clients, however you define them) will never experience this debate. They will make up their minds about the real thing, the product of the debate. The point is that the medium really is the message. Disney's message was the wondrous power of animals like the tiger. Debate got nowhere until the medium changed to 'Tiger'! Similarly with the credit card story, we could have talked all day, trying to picture a consumer's reaction to the new cards. But it was only when we changed the medium and made it 'real' that the new card literally came alive.

Let's leave the world of business briefly and think about people we all consider to be highly creative – artists and inventors. Have you ever heard of an artist writing a report to explain his work? He leaves that to the critics while he gets on with creating. How about an inventor? He produces a prototype – a word we are going to use a lot more of in this chapter. It may be made from cardboard and held together with an elastic band, but it's a prototype all the same. He instinctively knows that the act of making it real, rather than writing a memo, will make the idea better and help convince himself and others that it is possible.

The saying that a picture is worth a thousand words is very true for creative behaviour. The beauty of a song or a picture is that it conveys the real essence of the idea and impacts deeply on our imagination. It 'touches us'. Literature aside, words are middle men. Someone could describe a painting by Van Gogh to you if you hadn't seen it, but it's a poor substitute for experiencing the real thing with your own eyes. The same applies to creative interchanges.

In this chapter we'll look at the exciting and enlightening world of realness.

'What I hear I forget, what I see I remember, what I do I know.'
Chinese proverb

Why words fail us

The Western education system is based primarily on words. From an early age we are encouraged to draw, sing and act at school, but these make up a tiny part of the curriculum compared to words. By the time we leave school our success is often judged solely on our ability to communicate using language.

Like many of the other behaviours mentioned in this book, this has enormous advantages for business. However when it comes to creativity we have found that words fail us dramatically. They do so for three reasons.

1. Theatre of the mind

When we are communicating simple facts and figures, words are an efficient way of ensuring everyone understands the same basic information simply and quickly. However, when we start to try to describe creative concepts our words are open to interpretation. That's the beauty of radio or books. We all interpret the story differently. We all get it but we all get it differently. We have a genuine theatre inside our heads – each of us seeing and feeling things differently. (Remember from Chapter 1 how the brain classifies according to past experience? Past experience affects what we see in our mind's eye.)

So, if I'm trying to get you to help build or even buy into my idea and all I'm doing is showing you a chart with a few bullet points, then I'm reducing the chances that you will 'get it'. I have no guarantee that the image forming in your head is the same as the one I'm trying to communicate. What makes this all the more tricky is that when I explain my idea, I don't know whether you're reacting to what I meant or to your interpretation of it. Using words as a creative medium can cause ideas to die at the first hurdle – people either don't get it or they get the wrong thing. Catch yourself next time you hear this: 'Oh is that what you meant – I thought you meant ...'

2. Insider-speak

Most successful organisations have a language all of their own. Mix up a few of the chairman's favourite phrases, a hefty dose of TLAs (three letter acronyms), and a sprinkling of MBA speak, and what you have is a recipe for confusion. Along comes some keen newcomer eager to suck up the prevailing corporate culture and pretty soon he or she is mimicking the local lingo too. What you have is a cocktail of language that makes sense to those in the know but not to outsiders. And yet ultimately it's always outsiders we are selling to.

The effect of this corporate speak is slowly and subtly to disconnect the people on the inside (you) from the people on the outside (your customers). The more disconnected you become, the harder it is for you to empathise with your market and recognise new insights. Realness forces you to communicate in the same way as your consumers. It reconnects you with their world.

3. Brain styles

Finally, not everyone 'gets' information the same way. Research in the field of Neuro-Linguistic Programming (NLP) has shown that people can be divided into three sensory types: verbal, visual and kinesthetic. This means they have a bias to taking in and understanding information using words, pictures or actions respectively. Bias towards each of these three styles is split roughly equally within the adult population. So if your communication at work is based solely on words, then you're only using the favoured medium of a third of your audience. A third would have 'got it better' if you had literally painted a picture, and another third would have understood better if you'd got them to act out or try the experience.

> *'Jaw, jaw is a bore, bore.'*
> ?What *If!*

TLA mania

A sure sign that you've got your own corporate language is the dreaded three-letter acronym. TLAs are part of a corporate obsession with reducing everything to computer-like code. Your job title, meeting, part of building, market category – even your name is not safe from a corporate attack of the TLAs.

Have you ever received one of these?

To:	MK
From:	BN
cc:	HC/OL
Re:	MRS and GPR Q3

Please note, this meeting will be held in MR3. Also, due to AF the NAM will not be present. OL to brief outside the meeting. Thanks.

Brian.

What's happening here? Brian Nicholson is sending a memo to Mike King, and Henry Cooke and Oliver Laurence are copied. The memo invites them to hear a summary of market research (MRS) and a review of gross profit (GPR) made in July, August and September. Brian also asks Oliver to brief the national accounts manager later. It's a brief message and it's effcient, perfect for the ER world but too much of it and we start speaking and thinking in TLAs. And our customers don't!

The results of a words-only zone

You can begin to see the limitations of using words around creativity. But the penny has yet to drop in most businesses. Instead, verbal cleverness has become in many cases more important than the quality of the content.

'In most companies, people are rewarded for talking – and the longer, the louder, and the more confusingly, the better', observe Jeffrey Pfeffer and Robert Sutton, two professors at Stanford University in a recent article in *Harvard Business Review*.[2] They call this phenomenon 'Smart Talk', and it results in the 'Smart-Talk Trap'.

'Rare is the manager who presents a new strategy with a single slide and an idea that can be summarised in a sentence', note Pfeffer and Sutton. Rarer still is the manager who produces a prototype of an idea and lets it do the talking for him. In the corporate environment, managerial ability is often judged by the ability to talk smart, rather than by actually making things happen.

Sounding clever often involves being critical. (Interestingly, research suggests that people who take a negative stance often appear to be brighter than those who are positive.) This has a particularly insidious effect on innovation. The way companies are organised encourages bright people to apply their considerable intellects to sounding clever – and picking holes in everyone else's ideas. The result, say Pfeffer and Sutton, is companies that are 'filled with clever put-down artists' and '… paralysed by the fear and silence these people spawn'.

[2] Pfeffer, J. and Sutton, R., 'The Smart-Talk Trap', *Harvard Business Review*, May–June 1999.

What can realness do for creativity?

So far we've explored how 'word-only zones' can block creative behaviour. Now let's look at the other side of the coin: what realness can do for creativity. Once you unleash realness in your workplace, its natural affinity with creativity will become crystal clear. Believe us, once you try it you will never go back! But rather than asking you to take our word for it, we have outlined below the three core benefits that realness can bring to creativity at work.

1. Realness: the idea builder

We've already seen why words are not the best medium for explaining ideas to others in a way that ensures they really get it. When an idea starts to look like the 'real thing', it will evoke reactions that a written concept could not. The minute you get to play with something new ideas come tumbling out. 'I love it but it's bulkier

than I thought it would be.' 'It tastes great but at the price we're talking about there's not enough of it'. 'Ooh I'm disappointed, I imagined something else.' 'It's really cute – I just love it so much more than I thought I would!'

What's happening here? The prototype gets us feeling and speaking like consumers. We immediately start building and growing the idea in a way that we would not have been able to do unless we actually interacted with it in person. It forces us to examine previously unimagined details. This is important because with innovation, the devil is in the detail. Many a fine idea has failed because the product or service was just that little bit too big, slow, dull, expensive, or had some other obvious shortcoming that could have been rectified if it had been spotted sooner.

Effectively what prototyping does is give you a rich source of fresh insights to go away with and incorporate into your next prototype to drive the project forward.

2. Realness: the great momentum maker

The second way that realness benefits creativity is through momentum. As you will have gathered, the behaviour of realness is not for idle souls! In the next chapter we will explore the impact momentum has on innovation in detail. For now, just remember this point: prototyping is the equivalent of putting a stick of dynamite down your corporate pants! Sit back and wait for the reaction.

Once something begins to look real, it prompts comment from all parts of the organisation. People wake up and smell the reality. If it falls to them to make these ideas happen, their contribution to the innovation process increases. Where there was endless discussion, there will be action. That action may even include saying: 'No, the idea is not worth pursuing, let's stop the project now'. But having the courage to stop is just as important as accelerating innovation projects. Prototyping pushes you into action in one or other direction, and either way is better than apathy.

Black and Decker Paintmate

What would you get if you combined a vacuum cleaner, a garden hose, a two-litre cola bottle and a paintbrush? The answer is the first prototype of the Black and Decker Paintmate, an automatic paint system that feeds paint to the brush, and one of the world's biggest DIY launches. The original prototype proved to the team that the basic idea was sound and encouraged others to step in and support the venture.

---

3. Realness: bring your Kirk to work.

We are going to make this section real by referring to the cult sci-fi story Star Trek. So if you are not familiar with the original TV series grab your parent, child or neighbour and ask them about the creative behaviour of Captain Kirk and Mr Spock. No doubt they will tell you about Spock's cold calculating logic. And of Kirk's remarkable ability to run on gut feelings, of his emotional side and his

bravery. They may also tell you that the two of them made a great pair, very different but complementary.

We see a parallel in creativity. Put simply, Mr Spock would revel in ER situations – he is the RAIN master! – whereas Captain Kirk would thrive in the greenhouse. The thing about Kirk is that he is not afraid to show his feelings. His judgements come from an emotional place deep within him – something that Spock frequently finds hard to fathom.

It is this openness about feelings, especially when you can't explain why, that defines really successful innovation cultures. Think about it. Consumers don't always do things for logical reasons – they often make Kirk not Spock decisions.

Why has Volkswagen brought back the Beetle? Not because the 'Love Bug' is the best car in the world, but because as consumers we love the shape – and probably watched too many Herbie movies in our youth. But at work we often feel inhibited about revealing the Kirk inside us. Work is a place where Spock behaviour is approved of and Kirk behaviour often suppressed.

The point is that creativity, the greenhouse, operates on gut feel and emotional response. Spock can always shoot down a great but not fully formed idea. (Remember the picture: is it a weed or is it a flower?)

Outside of work, we're all consumers. We live in the 'real world', too. We have hobbies and passions that are reserved for leisure time. Many people find that the more ER-like work becomes, the more important non-ER activity outside of work is to them. The more you bury your head in the spreadsheet, the more you want to garden at the weekend.

Given a chance many of us like to cook, chop trees, refurbish the loft or make things with our hands. This hands-on thing is missing from most people's professional lives. To be encouraged to do it at work is highly fulfiling. Realness allows people to bring their Kirk persona into work. Suddenly, business is using the 'whole person'. It's literally 'hands-on' – and it's great fun.

'Dear friend, theory is all grey, and the golden tree of life is green.'
Johann Wolfgang von Goethe (1749–1832)

A real environment

There's no place like home, they say, and when it comes to the workplace nothing could be less true. Colourless, airless, artificially lit, grandiose glass offices or lowly rabbit hutches, power suits or dehumanising uniforms take over. Real life and real play it seems are put on hold.

The impacts for realness are tangible. First in the head. In an environment dominated by desks and computers, the chance to play and make things real diminishes. Chopping up boxes on the beautiful meeting room table, cooking up new food ideas at your desk. Don't think so. Second, the office separates us from our normal day-to-day lives, the way we live, how we mix, who we see.

Watch out for the next big leap in office design. Domesticised offices which reflect the way we live and give us room to play. It's already started. Take British Airways' new £200 million shopping mall-style business centre at Waterside near Heathrow. Complete with high street, pavement cafes, florist, library and supermarket. Where CEO Robert Ayling is frequently spotted in his pullover.

Or take Arthur Andersen, whose London office has different areas to encourage different sorts of working. A Zen ring for quiet thinking and a chaos room for teams to invent and play in.

So take a look, how much realness do you have around you?

Making realness happen

Realness is not a sophisticated science; it's more a mindset. It's about thinking 'How can I make this real now?' Below are our top six insights and observations on bringing realness into work.

1. Looping the loop

At ?What *If!*, we use the word 'prototyping' interchangeably with realness. For us, the beauty of prototyping is the unique role it plays in the creative process. Prototyping is not something you do at the end of a creative process, but is an integral part of that process. A common misconception is that making things real is the responsibility of a small group of people in an organisation, say product development. For prototyping read 'learning and inspiring by doing' – a skill we can all adopt, not something that marketing people hand over to implementation people. This misses the value of that all-important question, 'how can we make this real now?'

Prototyping means you quickly turn an idea – words and thoughts – into something real. A prototype is something you can touch, put in your pocket, play with in your hands. You can literally weigh it up. Prototypes are a fantastic way of evoking new insights and builds, and of checking what works and what doesn't. As soon as one prototype is finished and has been interrogated, a new one can be started. Skilled inventors know that the critical issue is how many of these loops they can pack in before launch. This means always asking this question early in the process: 'how can we make it real now?' But also following it up with a 'Quick, let's incorporate those insights and make it real again'.

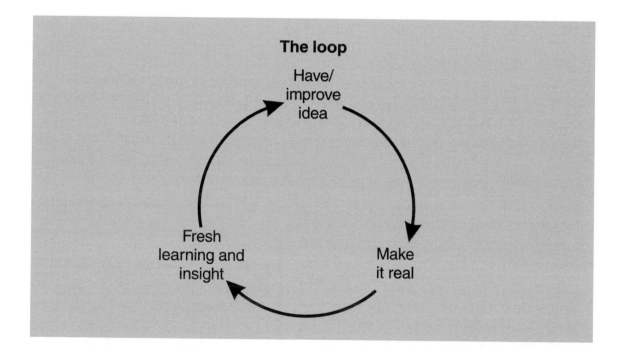

'If a picture's worth a thousand words, then a prototype is worth a million.'

Trevor Baylis, inventor of the clockwork radio

The point is that the real value comes from looping the loop. Using the experience and energy of one loop to drive the next. What's more it's an incredibly exciting and creative behaviour, challenging you to find new approaches and answers. In fact we often call it the 5th R (see freshness).

Dyson – 5127 loops

Today, James Dyson is regarded as one of Britain's leading entrepreneurs and inventors. The story of his 'dual cyclone' vacuum cleaner is the stuff of business legend. Dyson beat near bankruptcy to establish his factory in Malmesbury, Wiltshire, and become the UK market leader. Throughout it all, he has never lost sight of the importance of realness.

Dyson invented the bagless 'dual cyclone' vacuum cleaner in 1978, back when flared trousers were in fashion (the first time round). Like most overnight successes, it's been a long journey. Five long years and 5,127 prototypes later, his idea became a working model. But it was another ten years before the product reached the market.

In between, Dyson tried unsuccessfully to get backing from the leading manufacturers. It was an eye-opening introduction to the world of big business. His brush with the corporate world gave him important insights into the sort of management culture that prevailed in some large companies. He was determined that his own firm would be different.

When he finally launched in 1993, Dyson's first product, the DC01 turned the UK market for upright cleaners on its head. Just 23 months after its launch, his invention became Britain's best selling vacuum cleaner, overtaking sales of Hoover, Electrolux, Panasonic and Miele. It was followed in 1995 by the DC02, the company's cylinder cleaner, which achieved similar results.

Today, the distinctive yellow, grey and purple vacuum cleaners are to be found in homes the length and breadth of the country. Dyson remains wary of the corporate mindset, and ensures the company culture also stands out from the crowd. Memos are banned, because he says they are 'just a way of passing the buck'. He has an even lower opinion of email. 'The graphics are so appalling I just can't get interested enough to read them', he says.

Company employees must follow two rules: no smoking and no ties. (When he was trying to get financial backing for his invention, Dyson once told the board of a company on America's east coast that ties make you go deaf in your old age.)

A hands-on familiarity with the product, the company believes, means that employees are passionate. Every new employee – including the former trade minister Richard Needham when he joined the company as a non-executive director – spends the first day assembling one of the famous dual cyclone machines. They can then buy the fruits of their own labour for £20 and take it home for their own use.

Individuality is also a strong feature of the company's culture. The company has a slogan: 'We should be human beings not business people'. Many staff are recruited straight from university because their minds are open to new ideas and working methods.

> They are encouraged to be different as a matter of principle – it's part of what James Dyson calls his 'anti-brilliance campaign'. 'Very few people can be brilliant', he says. 'And they are overvalued. It's much more exciting to be a pioneer. Be a bit whacko and you shake people up. We all need shaking up.'[1]

2. Realness knows no limits

There are some forms of realness that are more apparent than others. We can all see how to mock up a new product but what about a service, or a meeting, or a conversation, or an internal process? Realness is just as applicable to services as to products. It's just that the methods may vary.

Take financial services for instance. You don't buy much of a 'thing', just benefits. You can't 'make' a new type of home mortgage. Or can you? We believe there is always a way. The key is to put yourself in consumers' shoes. Actors call this rehearsal or roleplay – the chance to experiment or explore something in real life not in words.

Let's imagine you are trying to prototype an innovative home mortgage. Why not mock up an advert for the mortgage and slip it into an appropriate magazine? Leave your colleagues to discover it. Or why not drill some independent financial advisors in the benefits of your home loan idea and have them role play trying to make some sales? This isn't market research. It's getting a close approximation of your idea out into the real world, instead of allowing it to languish on paper in some filing cabinet.

Some products are simple but rely on a complex ritual of use and appreciation. In these cases, there is all the more need to prototype, especially if the end-user is

[1] Dearlove, Des, 'Long road to a big clean-up', *The Times*, 30 July 1998.

very different to you. At ?What *If!*, we often ask our clients to act out or roleplay their brands rather than just talk to us about them. Try this, it works. Ask the members of your team to come to your next development meeting with a picture of someone from your target market pulled from a magazine. Then get them to introduce themselves as this person and tell the team about their life. Question them too. Make sure they stick to the first-person narrative. Ask them to give their opinion on your particular product development.

You will be amazed at the richness of information they provide. They'll tell you things that are all too easy to discount as unimportant when you are wrapped up in the corporate world. Remember it's only a prototype, don't worry about whether what they say is completely accurate. What counts is that they stimulate you to consider product improvements. The beauty of this prototyping is that it can be used to bring anything to life. For the courier example below we could easily have applied the same principles to prototype a new internal distribution system, a new management development review process, or any other internal process re-engineering initiative.

Delivering some realness

Some services are complex in their delivery. For instance, take the new wave of courier tracking systems that have been launched. Perhaps the big idea is to tell customers where their goods are, using a prerecorded message that literally telephones them to say where the parcel or package is in its journey. How would you prototype this?

You could find a large room, plenty of willing volunteers and turn your ideas into a mini play. Each volunteer could play the role of a part of the value chain. So someone could be the executive who wants to send a package; someone else the PA making the arrangements; someone else the courier company telephonist who takes the order; and so on. Don't worry you won't need the talents of Steven Spielberg to direct this production. In fact, why not run several versions of the play? You could give each version a title or scenario such as: 'Happy Customer'; 'Technology Failure'; 'Budget Version', 'Spot the Difference with the Competition'; and so on. The very act of walking through – in this case, acting through – each stage of the process and each scenario will force you to focus on the details of the idea.

The question is always the same and repeats like a mantra in the head of the inventor: 'How can I make it real right now?' Always ask yourself this question of your creative tasks.

3. Realness at home
Realness is a powerful tool for creative internal change as well as for product and service innovation. If you have an idea for changing how things are at work, get on and 'make it real now'.

One of the most common areas for internal innovation is communicating more effectively. If you have an idea about a new type of meeting, don't wait to get agreement from all parties (you won't) just try it out. (Some of our experiments with meetings are described in the next chapter.)

If you want to get a feel early on in a project's life about what top management will say, why not pretend you are the board. Get someone to act out how the finance director will react, what the CEO will say and so on. The issue is the same – let's stop talking and make the experience real now.

4. Encourage imperfection

Never forsake realness for the sake of 'finishedness'. Prototypes are rough and ready. That's part of their charm. They are the best you can do with the time and available resources. If a prototype is too finished, it actually stops people from commenting. If it's that finished, they think, then it's no longer under development.

Your prototypes should shout out 'come and change me, don't leave me like this!' Remember that you will loop the loop over and over again with your prototypes. In the previous courier example if all the participants in the roleplay know they will produce say ten iterations of their plays, it will affect how they prototype. They know it's not the final version, so they will happily dive in and give it a go without worrying about making a fool of themselves.

This was brought home to us when we mocked up a completely new holiday brochure in under four hours! Previously, we had shown fully designed dummy brochures to two groups of consumers. We quickly realised that what we thought was a striking new brochure was just more of the same to our audience. So it was back to school time. With pens, crayons, pictures from magazines and scissors and a lot of glue, we cobbled together two very rough, but radically different designs. The level of finish was no higher than you'd expect from a group of 11-year-olds. But the next two consumer groups didn't care, they could see and talk about our new ideas, they were excited and could build on what we'd done. The prototypes became the tool through which a whole new direction emerged. It was a striking confirmation of realness rather than an obsession with perfection.

5. Share your realness

Don't lock your prototypes away – leave them lying about in your office. We guarantee your colleagues and your boss will be drawn to them like a moth to a flame. They'll leave notes on your desk with advice and praise. Even better your boss will steal your prototype and show it to his or her boss. Before you know it, your innovation project will have attracted attention and will have the heavy guns behind it. And all because you made it real.

Hewlett Packard has made this principle part of its culture. All technical staff are encouraged to have the latest prototype of the project they're working on sitting on their desk at all times. Colleagues can see how work is progressing and make comments and suggestions to improve it. The company also recognises that because staff are also consumers, it is a great way to get a consumer reaction as early as possible. It means that H-P employees don't think in abstract terms, but physical reality. They live with the product every day, just as the customer will.

6. Don't think, just leap

We can promise you that the first time you introduce realness at work not everyone will be happy to participate. There are always those who find the path less travelled an uncomfortable route (you know who they are). Do not give up. Just dive in and have a go. This is the very essence of creativity. Just do it. It will be hard at first but the benefits can only be experienced by doing it.

'Chop your own wood – it will warm you twice.'
Proverb

IDEO

The industrial product design firm IDEO is famous for its prototyping culture. Clients include some of the best-known computer companies and even the occasional Hollywood movie producer. The company helped create the very first Apple Computer mouse and the 25-foot mechanical whale in the 'Free Willy' films.

With offices in nine locations, and a string of world class clients, IDEO has built its reputation on prototyping. So potent have IDEO's creative juices proved that *Fortune* magazine described the company's seemingly chaotic design studio as 'one of Silicon Valley's secret weapons'. The secret of its own success, the firm believes, lies in its ability to sustain a culture of innovation.

So how do they do that? Despite the intense pressure and tight deadlines that are part and parcel of their jobs, the company maintains an air of creative anarchy. IDEO prides itself on its prototyping environment. Staff are encouraged to 'play' at work, and the most important rule is – to break the rules.

Along with the last word in computer imaging, IDEO offices are literally strewn with cardboard, foam, wood and plastic prototypes. Staff work wherever they happen to be and scribbled notes are scattered all around. A 'cacophonous kindergarten classroom' is how management writer Tom Peters described it.

To the untrained eye it may look like a chaotic mess. But David Kelley, the company's founder and front man, describes the firm as 'a living laboratory of the workplace. The company is in a state of perpetual experimentation', he says. 'We're constantly trying new ideas in our projects, our work space, even our culture'.[2]

[2] Dearlove, Des, 'Innovation from the chaos', *The Times*, 30 July 1998.

Structuring for realness

We think that realness will become an increasingly important source of competitive advantage. We've come across a number of companies which already structure realness into the way they work. Below are some examples.

Van den Bergh: your desk in a kitchen

If you work in a food company shouldn't you work in a kitchen? That was the thought behind Van Den Bergh Holland's decision to build a completely new food development facility.

Integrating marketing and R&D, the centre is purpose built to put food at the centre of all activities. The new facility contains fully functioning kitchens, development laboratories and teaching centres as well as the basic workplace requirements of desks and chairs. Throw into the pot consumer workshops, food demonstrations, cookery courses and visiting chefs and the company bubbles with realness.

Keep clients waiting

London advertising agency Saatchi and Saatchi used realness to great effect in winning the pitch for the British Rail advertising business. Senior rail executives were kept waiting outside the meeting until they reached breaking point and got ready to leave. At this point the team stepped in, explaining that these were the same feelings rail customers felt for the notoriously erratic train service and went on to deliver advertising which sought to address this issue. Once the nerves had calmed the business was won.

People's Bank: don't debate it – test it

People's Bank has a refreshingly original attitude to new ideas. 'Don't debate it, test it' is one of the key philosophies of this innovative American financial services organisation. Fed up with endlessly debating whether an idea was a winner or loser and learning little along the way, the bank shifted its paradigm to a 'test it before you judge it' approach. The result is an organisation dedicated to making new ideas real as quickly as possible then piloting them in managed circumstance to check the appeal and improve the idea.

Next: what's next?

Leading UK fashion retailer Next is renowned for its high quality, simple and innovative shop layouts with each new season of clothes. Probe for the secret of its consistent success and you discover that back at HQ is a full size mock up of a high Street shop. This way buyers, designers and merchandisers are forced to not just buy the clothes, but look at how the new ranges live and feature in the real shopping environment.

With these sorts of structures you can return to your inventive roots. Rather than feeling frustrated, you can get your hands dirty and start to give life to your ideas.

'When in doubt make it real. (You'll soon know if there is hope.)'
?What *If!*

Realness with consumers

The world of market research would learn much from realness.

Market research has driven a huge wedge between the consumer and the provider. Ever more complicated techniques mean we spend our time reading the report rather than making consumer experiences real.

This isn't to say that we don't value market research. It's just that we believe it should be complemented by real experience. (How many of you are your target market?)

Over the last few years we've:

• Hired a street for the day to immerse an R&D department in the consumer's world.

• Had the board of a company present its five-year plan to consumers.

• Been to breakfast with a different family every day of the week.

• Had consumers conduct a cost reduction exercise rather than the technical teams.

None of this was meant to replace market research. But what it did do was give us the real experience from which to grow and develop our thinking. So next time you look at your research budget consider some consumer realness.

Summary

Realness at work means that you stop talking and stop sending memos. It means that you ask yourself a simple question: 'How can I make this real right now?'

The aim is to find a way of reproducing the experience you were so busy talking about, and bring the idea to life.

For lots of organisations, this goes against the grain. They have created 'word-only cultures'. Realness involves a revolution in the way we behave at work.

The benefits are better ideas, more momentum and greater fulfilment at work.

Do it early and see how many times you can loop the loop.

Don't be a perfectionist.

Share your prototypes.

Just do it now.

Go on!

Creative Behaviour Four

Momentum

Why is it that having great ideas isn't the hard part of innovation?
It's 'making them happen' that hurts.

Is this you?

You have lots of great ideas but find it's a struggle to make them happen.

You suffer from death by diary – you hold a brainstorm, but when you arrange the follow-up no one can make it for several weeks.

You are so busy (running around keeping all your projects on the go) that you can't find time to really get stuck into any one of them.

You feel like you spend most of your energy battling with the company and its systems instead of the competition.

You talk eloquently about the state of your projects but aren't really passionate about any of them.

You are working on projects that have been floating around the business for ages.

Momentum: The quantity of motion of a moving body, measured as a product of its mass and velocity.
Source: *Oxford English Dictionary*

Momentum: The management of personal, team and corporate energy to ensure that innovation happens.
Source: ?What *If!*

What is momentum?

Have you ever watched kids at play? They have a focus and intensity about them that seems to shut out everything else. The cardboard box (the one that the dishwasher came in) is really a boat. The kids are rushing around collecting provisions for their voyage. Interrupt their mission to give them a meal, and they stop just long enough to wolf it down. Then they're off again – back to the boat. Now they're rigging up a sail from a broom handle and an old sheet. There is a speed and happy spontaneity to their play. This is momentum.

In the business world most of us can conjure up an image of Bill Gates and his partner Paul Allen battling it out in the early days of Microsoft. Lots of late nights. Lots of caffeine. Lots of take-out pizza. Did they even notice the time? Probably not. That's what happens when a team is pulling in the same direction. They were

on a mission, personally motivated and exhilarated by the same goal. Lots of laughter; lots of setbacks. This, too, is momentum. Momentum is all about getting on and doing whatever you have to do to make something happen. It's not about taking small bites out of a task whenever time permits. It's about really getting your teeth into it and wrestling it to the floor. It's the fourth behaviour of creative people.

Think of momentum as an unreasonable sense of urgency and a clarity of direction. It's a behaviour all great creative leaders have. (They can be frustrating at times, infuriating even, but life is never dull around them.) Skilled innovators instinctively know how to create this state. They enthuse the people around them and create the running track to beat the competition.

What does momentum feel like?

So how does it feel to be working on a project with momentum? You can feel the positive buzz in the air. The presence of momentum charges the air like ionised particles. You can spot it a mile away. When a project really catches fire, it's as obvious as seeing a light bulb come on. There is an energy and optimism about people that is infectious. There is a palpable sense of determination to get the job done, no matter what obstacles get thrown in the way. The team has a purpose. Team members know what they have to do and why it's valuable to them and their company.

Teams like this will also have a manager who understands that if the energy starts to fall away inertia can take hold. Inertia is the arch-enemy of momentum. If an innovation project is worth doing, it's almost always worth doing quickly.

To us, momentum is the same thing as the management of human energy. The trouble is that most managers don't consciously manage this aspect of their work. 'Energy management' is understood at an intuitive level, and practised instinctively by some people. But it is not yet established as a legitimate business skill. It's not something that's discussed so it remains in the shadows of business life.

Part of our creative revolution is a new way of understanding energy management or momentum at work. At present, few companies distinguish between good energy-momentum, which is vital to innovation, and bad energy-momentum, the unplanned urgency and crises associated with emergency room (ER) situations. The effects are there for all to see. Massive stress as the company lurches from one mini-crisis to the next and organisations that are full of unfinished projects getting passed from one department to another because no one will admit they've stalled. No one will take responsibility to drive them through or pull the plug.

We choose how to use our time in our daily jobs. To speed things up in one area, something has to slow down somewhere else. That's the reality of business life. But be warned, momentum is much more than just a fancy word for time management.

We believe energy management must be legitimised and brought out into the open. In this chapter we examine the worlds of '*can't* companies' and '*can* companies'. We will explore the barriers to momentum that *can't* companies erect. As ever, we will focus on solutions. First, practical energy management techniques, and second, what we call the 'hard edge of creativity' – understanding what really motivates us at work and how we can take personal responsibility for making things happen.

'If you really want to kill an idea, do it slowly!'
?What *If!*

Can and can't companies

We've seen enough companies to know that some are much better at getting things done than others. The culture of a *can* company is very different to that of *can't* company. Let's look at *can* companies first. The first thing you notice is the buzz. People look happy and busy. Team members know what success is, and why it's important. They're also clear that they have to deliver it – that the buck stops with them. The success of a high-revving 'momentum' team inspires others. Word of momentum quickly spreads. The first success creates a feel-good factor, which has a ripple effect. Other teams copy the energetic approach. Before long people find themselves looking at their company and feeling pretty good. 'Yes we can do this', they say; 'we can do that, too'. The business develops a head of steam. Now it's really moving. Momentum is a very visible behaviour.

Can cultures have a confidence about them that inspires staff to try new things, safe in the knowledge that their company is the sort of company that *can* do things. They draw confidence from the fact that their company has a track record of pushing ideas through the system and implementing them. Everyone in a *can* culture knows their efforts won't be wasted.

The reason momentum plays such a key role in *can* cultures is clear when you break down the innovation process into its three component parts. The three Is of innovation are:

Insights + Ideas + Implementation = Innovation

We call this the 'Innovation Equation'. It recognises that unless creative ideas are based on a real insight and get to see the commercial light of day, they don't benefit the business. They may be great fun, but they are little more than entertaining distractions.

Momentum connects up the three Is. It's the driving force behind extracting and improving ideas (remember looping the loop in realness) and getting on and making them happen. Momentum is what underpins the culture of *can* companies.

Momentum is also key to creativity because it's fun! Creative fact of life number 1: ideas rarely come if you have a frown on your face. They come if you have a smile, and they come with passion. Anything is possible if you have a levity of spirit and a good sense of humour – or if you really care and are determined to make something happen. We know of no other way.

So what about *can't* companies? How does it feel to work for one, and why don't they have the momentum to get things done? *Can't* companies feel very different to their *can* counterparts. The energy and optimism needed to push innovation through just doesn't exist. We've had clients tell us they 'just know that this organisation won't get it's act together and do something'. This low level of corporate self-esteem is a prime creativity killer.

Inspiring individuals to contribute innovative ideas on a regular basis goes hand in hand with demonstrating momentum. If you believe your company will make it happen, you are far more likely to contribute your creativity to the innovation process. In *can't* companies the reverse is true.

Without careful management, the forces of inertia within a company can fester into fact. Pretty soon it becomes part of the corporate mythology that the board will not take risks. This is something we find perplexing as we are often briefed by senior managers who complain that junior staff do not present them with provocative or risky plans.

You may see a little of both the *can* and *can't* in your business, but overall which label fits your company best? Is yours a *can* or *can't* company? If you're in the first camp, great – but you can always get better. If you're in the latter camp, let's have a quick look at how you got in this state by looking at four basic barriers to momentum in *can't* cultures.

The four barriers to momentum

Barrier 1: growth without energy management

In a small business, maintaining momentum is much easier. There are few people to create bottlenecks, fewer systems to get in the way, less need for planning. Often these businesses have that magical 'start up' energy and an attitude that anything is possible, 'let's just give it a go'.

But as companies become bigger they begin to lose these energising momentum factors, sometimes without realising it. Systems can all too easily get out of control and start to take over. What once was a coffee machine huddle is now an extended and bureaucratic approval process. There are so many people to keep in the loop that innovation leaders spend more time making sure that everyone is informed and consulted than actually having new ideas and driving projects.

As businesses grow they hunger for predictability. The bigger they get, the hungrier they become. With size and success comes responsibility to shareholders and staff. It's natural, then, that big business wants to plan and manage the future as precisely as the clock ticks a new day.

Unfortunately, momentum doesn't fit neatly into this scheme of things. It upsets the predictable beat of the planner's clock. By its very nature momentum behaviour is often unplanned. It demands that we follow where our passion leads us. We only really know how hard to push once a project is in motion. You can't plan it in advance.

These three factors then – the growth of systems, increasing numbers of people and the demands for planning – have an enormously negative effect on your company's ability to keep momentum. We wouldn't be surprised if you had predicted all three factors. However, there is a repercussion that receives very little attention: the deliberate management of energy and emotion. This again is a factor of growth. Big business finds it hard to maintain an intimate (almost family) feel. The common spirit and passion that binds a small group of people together is replaced by a salary structure and a promotion system. Over time, these competitive arenas become the last place people want to show emotions in.

Most managers are just not aware of how to recognise when momentum is needed, and feel uneasy about 'managing' someone else's energy or emotion. (We use the words emotion and energy interchangeably here, as the former drives the latter.) This comes from a fear that in confronting the emotional aspects of work we may reveal too much about ourselves, and intrude on the private lives of others. It's easier to hide behind a mask of professionalism.

At the moment, lots of potential 'energy managers' out there feel that work is work – a place to get the job done. After work, they tell themselves, we are free to be who we really want to be. So why interfere? This is fine up to a point, but it creates an obstacle to introducing creativity and innovation into the workplace.

The myth that business isn't meant to be fun, that good business is serious business, has done more to suppress momentum than any other single factor. We started this chapter with a reference to children playing – there are many who find other people's enthusiasm at work 'childish'. We reject this notion. Emotion, enthusiasm, energy, passion, whatever you call it – it's the lifeblood of innovation.

Too many managers have erected barriers to protect themselves from these very emotions. We believe that, in time, creative revolutionaries will swarm over this barricade. They will demand to know why emotions are excluded from a large proportion of people's lives. They will throw off the chains traditional managers have shackled themselves and others with.

Yes, we are passionate about this. Passionate and proud of it. If it makes you uncomfortable, then maybe you're not ready for the next step. Maybe you aren't ready to unleash the forces of creative momentum in your organisation. With it comes additional responsibility to be aware of the energy and emotions of those you want to inspire. The management of energy requires the encouragement of passion and commitment, not relying on the old corporate hierarchy of fear and promotion.

Barrier 2: the innovation rollercoaster

Asking people at work to be productively creative, to be innovative, is to ask them to do a fundamentally difficult job. What we mean by asking someone to take the job of innovation director is to ask him or her to challenge the system, try new things – and expensive, risky ones at that.

The innovation director won't have a lot of ammunition to take up the good fight with. He will often have to argue from a position of gut feel, not fact (Kirk not Spock), have little resource and be surrounded by a mixed audience, some open and some sceptical. Daniel, welcome to the lion's den! Perhaps life is kinder to innovators in your organisation – if so, you are exceptional. The barriers most innovation managers will experience will not be apparent at the start of an innovation project. Starting a project is like rolling a ball downhill. People love to escape the ER environment for a while and let their hair down in the greenhouse. Creative sessions are a welcome break from almost any job. People revel in their new-found freedom to challenge accepted wisdom. These are the heady early days of an innovation project when anything seems possible. It's like being 18 years old again and it's Friday night!

The honeymoon period doesn't last long. The reality is that there are a lot of knocks in store along the way. The almost naively optimistic energy of the initial (downhill) stage can go one of two ways. Either it will begin to falter and eventually stall, or it will become the freight train of momentum. Much depends on the skill of the leader.

The following are nine great examples of uphill stages of an innovation rollercoaster:

1. At the end of the creative session someone takes the notes to type. When you eventually see them again they communicate none of the excitement you felt at the meeting.

2. Halfway through a project, you discover there are no funds available to support the product launch.

3. Your technical colleagues shake their heads and say 'it can't be done'.

4. Your project always seems to be the last thing on your list of things to do.

5. The finance director asks for rock solid facts about how much of this new idea you will sell.

6. The board suffers collective memory loss and forgets why it was a good idea in the first place.

7. Your team don't call you anymore to tell you what they think you should do next.

8. Key supporters leave.

9. You hear that a competitor is about to launch the same thing.

To keep the momentum going the project leader will have to muster the extraordinary energy required to overcome uphill setbacks and marshal the passion and support of the team to push the project through. Unless we successfully manage our own energy, and that of our team, through this rollercoaster of an innovation ride, how can we expect our people to have another go? After a knock-back, they have to be able to pick themselves up, dust themselves down and find the steely determination to keep going.

Momentum makes a difference for Bass

A drinks industry story illustrates what a little momentum can do. In the mid-1990s, the CEO of Bass Brewing UK was visiting Australia where he came across a new product from a local brewing company. It was alcoholic lemonade – a product that didn't exist in the UK. Recognising its potential, he returned home with a mission to launch the new product.

Back in the UK, Bass managers realised that it was only a matter of time before the competitive product was launched in their home market. They knew, too, that the first brand to hit the streets stood the best chance of capturing market leadership. The only trouble was that the competition already had a fully developed version. Bass didn't.

What the company did next goes to show what can be achieved with sufficient momentum and resources. In just 12 weeks, Bass developed and launched its own product, Hooch. It became the number one seller in the UK, with Two Dogs, the Australian rival, a distant second. However, the momentum didn't stop here. Over the course of the next two years, the brand became a national favourite, successfully launching three new flavours and special editions at Christmas (Ho Ho Hooch) and St Valentines Day (Smooch). A new way of behaving for a traditional beer company.

Barrier 3: bar coding time

We call the third barrier to momentum 'bar coding' time. It's the great management disabler of our age, and we're all guilty of it to a greater or lesser extent. It involves the habit of managing as many things as you can in a day, working in hourly chunks (sometimes even smaller) without ever really having the time to focus on one project with any real intensity.

A day in our working life  stop, start, stop, start ...

What we do is slice the working day into as many slivers of time as possible and use them to cover as many tasks as we can. You can imagine looking at a busy manager's diary and seeing a bar code! Managers are literally spreading themselves too thinly in a desperate attempt to do too much. The effect is that they don't ever give a decent push to any one project. Is your diary a bar code diary?

Most time management systems seem to pander to this. They focus on helping the modern manager to juggle as many activities in one business day as is humanly possible. (And haven't we become good at it!)

Bar coding time kills creativity. You may feel like Superman because you have managed to keep so many balls in the air, but the plain fact is that creativity requires a passion for the subject. Lots of short meetings mean you have to fall in love with your task all over again every time you come back to it.

In this way bar coding time drains the build up of momentum and siphons off enthusiasm. The original passion for the project may be rediscovered towards the middle or end of each mini session, but it's lost by the time of the next session. Time is wasted getting momentum back again. Contrary to popular belief, at work absence does not make the heart grow fonder, it just makes it forget.

How many times have you heard or said yourself, 'Hurry up, let's finish the agenda, I've got a plane to catch'. Momentum thrives on the kind of energy created when people have a get together and relax. They need to toy with new ideas, to let the forces of serendipity work their magic, and weave their spell. Shooting the breeze is a legitimate innovation tool.

Is it any wonder that so many of the executives we talk to speak of a soulless existence at work? Bar coding time misses the point about how humans invent. We work best when we pursue our passion.

Barrier 4: the split inventor syndrome
The fourth major barrier to momentum is what Dublin-based consultant and writer Sandy Dunlop calls the 'split inventor syndrome'. Large businesses tend to split the inventing process into functional parts. Those responsible for the original insight are unlikely to be the same people who will commercialize the idea.

Innovation doesn't work this way. Look at great innovators and you'll find that most work alone or in small teams. They keep things tight. They are involved in all aspects of the innovation, not just their particular skill set. If they are not expert then they become expert or they find an expert. They don't hand the idea over to another set of people who have not been involved from the start. Inventors know they will have to stick with the project to the end and accept the consequences personally.

But when we look at large companies, what do we find? Most companies organise a phased approach to innovation, with one department passing on to another at different stages of a project. It is still very rare to have a single champion from inception to launch. Moreover, it is still fairly common for companies to have different locations for different functions. This just exacerbates the split inventor issue further. Some companies are now getting wise to at least the disadvantages of disparate locations but we're still a long way from having real personal ownership for projects in most businesses.

Unified inventors

When it designed a new R&D facility, the German carmaker BMW went out of its way to overcome split inventor syndrome. Rather than divide them up along functional lines, all those contributing to a new model are physically located in the same area.

The company worked out which people needed to communicate most frequently and built that into the office layout. So development design staff are situated next to their related production planning colleagues. All design offices are located on the same floors as their model workshop. The aim is to allow people working on the same project to communicate with each other by the shortest possible route.

Creating momentum

So where are we up to? So far we have discussed what momentum is, how it drives *can* companies and what stops it in *can't* companies. We have seen that momentum is about energy, and energy management. Think of it as an energy balance as in the picture below. The balance of energy can tip either way. In *can* companies it tips to create momentum. In *can't* cultures it tips to create inertia. Organisations that keep working to create momentum can sustain it for years. At a corporate level momentum can often manifest itself as that 'winning feeling'. You just know that if anyone can do it and do it first then it's going to be your organisation. That feels great and is felt at all levels. It sounds corny but everybody wants to be part of the winning team.

The force of momentum is made up of passion, enthusiasm and emotional openness. The force of inertia is caused by unfocused energy – you may still be busy and will more likely be quite stressed, but your energy is being dissipated in many directions and blocked by opposing forces.

So following this simple model, to increase momentum we have two choices. We can either reduce inertia causing activities or encourage greater momentum. Of course these forces work against each other. Momentum is the antidote to inertia.

We are going to show you how to remove barriers and push down inertia later. First we are going to explore how aligned energy is the key to motivation and momentum.

Alignment and momentum

The primary thing that drives momentum is alignment. Before you embark on a voyage of innovation, check whether you have it or not. Ensure all participants, from the top to the bottom, internal and external, want similar things.

Let's look first at an organisation that does not have alignment. Imagine a business that has a few clear goals but communicates them poorly to employees. Or a business that communicates its goals well but there are so many of them that few are remembered. Under such a regime it's not difficult to justify the existence of almost any project. After a while cracks in the system appear as an unwieldy number of initiatives vie for limited funds. Lots of energy is expended on internal debate. The ensuing infighting drains the energy for 'outfighting' with the competition.

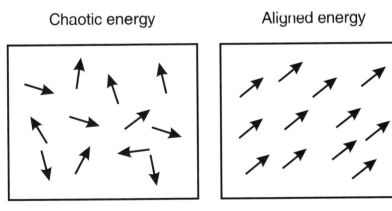

Chaotic energy   Aligned energy

Bad busy   Good busy

Chaos kicks in when employees' motivations and goals are not aligned to those of the business. At some point in the innovation process someone will crack under the pressure and think: 'No, I don't want to do this enough to keep working so hard'. They may tell you this or they may keep it to themselves. Working at half throttle, not willing to take risks or to go the extra mile, these people may put on a pretence of momentum, but their heart isn't in it. (They are not always easy to spot.)

The result of this misalignment is confused or even chaotic energy, rather than aligned energy. The sensation can be likened to a misfiring engine. It isn't like the smooth purr of human horsepower that comes with alignment. You find yourself devoting more time to looking out for members of the team who are either not interested or not performing. You begin to lose your sense of direction on a project and end up going down blind alleyways.

Before long you and certain team members are running around like the proverbial headless chickens. You're not being lazy; you are just misdirecting and ultimately wasting energy. Although people look busy they're just chasing their tails. The result is a gradual falling off of momentum as the forces of inertia take hold, and eventually the project stalls. We've all seen it happen many times. What, then, are some of the characteristics of a team lacking alignment?

1. Your project team starts to disagree on what priority the project has in the wider scheme of company priorities.

2. Some of your team, while they were enthusiastic to begin with, seem to have lost their power to 'self-start'.

3. Team members start to question why they are bothering with the project at all.

4. You hear about initiatives sanctioned by the board that seem to be at odds with what you thought were your project's goals.

5. Privately, some members of your project team complain to you about other members. Why are they on the team? What added value do they bring?

6. You don't look forward to team meetings.

A project with alignment looks very different. Here are some key characteristics of an aligned team. Do you recognise times when you have been in this type of team?

1. Everyone knows what the judgement criteria is that will be used to assess the project.

2. They understand how the project fits in the company's wider strategic objectives – team members can easily gauge its importance.

3. Everyone knows how important the project is compared to all the other work they have to do – they can prioritise for themselves.

4. The focus is on achieving the goals – not internal politics (outfighting not infighting).

5. Your team feels 'together' and supportive – they're buzzing.

6. The members of your team don't just understand the objective itself, they understand the intent. They can answer the question 'why are we doing this?' They can answer it straightaway, and without any prompting.

This list summary is helpful as a simple diagnostic to establish the levels of alignment in your team. Once you have this awareness, the next step is to decide what you are going to do about it.

There are broadly two appraches, depending on the scale of change or seriousness of the problem. First, we'll examine a short-term strategy and then a longer-term approach designed to change behaviour.

'A match of corporate and individual souls releases those "E" factors (energy, enthusiasm, effort, excitement, excellence).'
Charles Handy

Short-term alignment

Creating a crisis

Have you ever tried to put a presentation together against the clock? You can almost guarantee a catalogue of disasters. First the printer runs out of ink, then the photocopier jams and of course you discover half the pages have been bound upside down. Sound familiar? What happens next? People rally round. They drop what they are doing and muck in. Somehow it all gets sorted in the end. You rush off with perfect documents, thanking everyone profusely whilst cursing the photo-copier which seems to have a personal vendetta against you.

In those few precious minutes of photocopier hell there was perfect alignment. Your goal was the same as everyone else's. There was no time for politics or debate, only one thing mattered.

Crises can provide real alignment, which tilts the balance in favour of momentum. Sometimes you can create a crisis to provoke alignment – but only when the deadlines are real. Too often businesses cry wolf, expecting people to drive projects forward to meet deadlines that have little real meaning. You can't spend all your time in crisis. You need the rest and space that comes with comfort. But as a short-term way to create momentum, crisis can be highly effective. Here are a couple of 'create a crisis' stories to make you smile.

Virgin's cola crisis

Virgin Cola grew out of the development of a premium cola formula by a Canadian company called Cott. Cott had come to the UK in the mid-1990s and had already launched a number of own-label cola brands for supermarket chains such as Safeway. The company was interested in launching a branded cola, so it approached Virgin's Richard Branson.

Branson and a member of his design team met with the company and were interested in the idea. They mocked up a few cans to see how they looked. After discussion with only a few employees, the Virgin chairman decided to go ahead.

His main concern was the level of come-back that Pepsi and Coca-Cola would be able to afford to mount. Against these two giants, he believed his only chance of getting ahead was to take them by surprise. That way they wouldn't have time to put big defensive plans in place.

In the UK, he went on *News at Ten*, ITN's flagship television news programme, to announce to the world his intention to launch a cola in just eight weeks time, despite never having made a drink before. At that moment, no more than a handful of Virgin employees had any clue about his plans. So it came as just as much of a surprise to them as it was to his competitors.

By creating a 'crisis', Branson forced his people to be very creative about the launch. The momentum was generated by the need for speed, and the cola was somehow launched within the seemingly impossible eight-week window.

A little white lie!

A large multinational confectionery and drinks company asked us to help its sales managers identify new promotional activities. We organised a brainstorming session in the back room of a local pub to greenhouse ideas. The participating managers duly arrived armed with a list of ideas they felt had real potential to move the business forward.

We developed some of these and then moved into the next phase, timetabling the actions. The managers found it hard to make the time to keep up the momentum on the projects. All complained that they were already heavily committed. Diaries were consulted. Excuses made. Regret expressed. But despite much cajoling from us, the schedule they came up with was pretty undemanding. Spread over the next 12 months, the projects had little chance of catching fire, and would probably wither and die.

At the next session we disingenuously introduced a new incentive. We cooked up a story about a fax from a competitor that had been found in the car park of a supermarket chain, one of their leading customers. We persuaded their boss to play along, and tell them that the competitor was working on some similar initiatives and had ambitious plans to launch its new product range within six months. Suddenly the atmosphere in the room changed. A number of those present suspected it was a put-up job, but one manager in particular responded in deadly earnest. His reaction was infectious. The managers now responded to what they saw as a competitive threat.

Diaries were reconsulted. Excuses were brushed aside. Regret was transformed into enthusiasm. After some discussion, they concluded that there was, after all, some space to move the schedule forward. They could mobilise their resources to get the ideas actioned. No problems!

The point of this story isn't to criticise these managers or their company. Once the challenge was set before them, they rose to it magnificently. Rather, the story serves to illustrate what happens at companies all the time. Innovation is seen as a long-term pay-off, when it should be seen as the key to competitive position. As a result, it is hard to get people to make the time and space in their schedules to create the momentum that is necessary to beat the competition to the punch.

What both these stories illustrate is that we can always do much more than we expect in much less time. We can proactively and positively choose more of our crises and use them to create the momentum so important to creativity and innovation.

Long-term behaviours

The hard edge of creativity

Creating a crisis is obviously a short-term strategy. So what of the longer term? How can you ensure alignment becomes an enduring state of affairs at work?

Start by checking that your team or organisation has set a limited number of crystal clear objectives, which have then been communicated over and over again throughout the organisation. If you want to find out if the message has got through, take a poll across the organisation and ask people to describe the aims of the business. (Unless the receptionist is clear about what's important, then the message hasn't got through.)

Once clarity and communication are in place, the real work begins. The next step is to motivate people to really take responsibility for making the vision a reality. They will only do this if you can illustrate how the team objectives dovetail with their own passions and goals. This is where one of those inescapable and hard-edged truths comes into play. Ask yourself: *'Am I really ready to take on this completely different way of working?'*

It's a question about our willingness to take personal responsibility, to look honestly at ourselves and figure out what our motivations really are. How do they line up with the project? Do I want these things as much as the company does? Am I in the same place as my colleagues? In Chapter Six we discuss the creative behaviour of bravery. One of the bravest things any of us can do is get to grips with what our true motivations in life are. For some people it can mean admitting all sorts of uncomfortable truths.

Personal motivation is directly linked to personal goals. The closer a project is aligned to your personal values and objectives, the more energy and momentum you have to give. If you really want to be more innovative, then you have to take this next step – and you have to be prepared to take the responsibility that goes with it. What can an organisation do to support this behaviour? Without organised support lots of new ideas and the energy that has gone into creating them will be wasted. Life's too short to just try harder. Make a structural change instead! What this means is that if we really want to change behaviours, we recognise that we must change people roles or create structures that support teams to adopt new behaviours.

Here are some examples of structures we've found useful for momentum. Some of them may work for you.

The buck stops here

One solution is to put a single person in charge of an innovation project. It may seem blindingly obvious but we have found the buck always gets passed up or down. Sooner or later a senior person is in hot water over something they had no idea about – or vice versa with a junior person. We need a revolution in the way we attribute responsibility. Making a single person responsible regardless of chain of command is a good start.

Objectives cascade

Procter & Gamble has a great system for managing alignment. It starts at the very top. The CEO publishes his Objectives, Goals, Strategies and Measures (OGSM). His immediate reports base their targets on the CEO's. In this way a single person can cascade his or her will throughout a vast organisation.

Do you take this project?

Make people stand up and take responsibility. We have a box called the Off Your Chest box. When it fills we gather everyone together and read out the contents. We have a rule: someone has to take personal responsibility for implementing a suggestion and they nominate themselves in this meeting. They signal their intent 'I will' loudly and clearly for all to hear. If no one volunteers to take the project forward then and there it instantly dies.

Ideas and impact

The brewing company Bass named its innovation change programme 'Ideas and Impact'. It sends a clear signal that ideas are useless without momentum (impact). One of the quickest ways to change a culture is by changing its language. After such a name change can you imagine Bass managers entertaining an idea without impact?

Our belief is that it's imposible in a large organisation for alignment to exist on it's own. The alignment structures are a powerful way of supporting a culture towards a common set of goals necessary for momentum. Without them the chances of strong alignment are much lower.

Reducing barriers to momentum

Let's imagine we've done all we can to create alignment and momentum, but we're still not really getting the level of response we'd like. The next stage is to examine the left side of the energy balance. How can we lower the barriers to momentum, and so reduce the forces of inertia? Doing too much is one of the biggest barriers to momentum. So when things slow down we always look to clear out excess in one of four areas.

1. Cut down projects

There is nothing new in saying 'do less'. 'Less breadth, more depth' is a common message most of us have heard, agreed with, and often spectacularly failed at.

'Put the big rocks in the jar first' goes the time management story. Our time is of course limited; there is only so much time you can put in a jar! If you fill the jar with all the little rocks first there will be no room for the big ones later. It's pretty obvious. But there's a big difference between common sense and common practice.

Why do so few of us manage to focus on just the big rocks? Our observation is that most of us don't take the time to pause and really sort out the big rocks (the important projects) from the small ('nice to do' but potential time wasters). Instead, we just tend to accept that they are all big – we view everything we're working on as vital.

How can we tell which are genuinely small rocks, the ones we could relatively easily discard with no real impact on the business or our own goals? To answer this question we need to figure out what we really want to get out of life at work.

But looking into ourselves and identifying what is and isn't important involves a degree of introspection that we are not used to in work situations. Most people aren't even aware they need to do it. Moreover, there is real pain in choosing to focus on some projects over others. We'd all like to do everything and we can't – the jar has limited capacity. Saying 'no' to some projects hurts. But we've observed that successful innovators have a ruthless streak – they know how to say 'no'.

Saying 'No' at Apple.

When Steve Jobs returned to Apple as CEO he was shocked to find so many diverse projects underway. He decided to rationalise – to say 'no' to some projects. With Jobs back in charge, Apple narrowed its focus to just two types of computer user – the professional, and the home user; and focused its firepower on two types of hardware – desktop and mobile.

This meant the company effectively had only four projects to work on. The pain of this decision was to effectively cut out plenty of potentially lucrative markets. So was the pain worth it? The first result of Apple's new-found focus was the fantastically successful iMac. Apple outsmarted the competition by bringing out a computer that not only had the Mac's legendary user-friendliness, but also looked completely different from all preceding computers. What was the secret of Apple's success? Because so few projects were now being worked on senior management could get much more involved in the detail of the ideas and decisions could be turned around in hours not weeks.

Bill Joy

Co-founder of Sun Microsystems, Bill Joy has been described as the 'Edison of the Internet'. *Fortune*[1] magazine recently noted that he is on 'a 20-year streak of innovation that has laid the groundwork for a new technological era.'

While still a student, Joy shaped AT&T's Unix operating system, which today is the main competitor to Microsoft's Windows. He's also credited with designing the most crucial circuits in Sun's SPARC microprocessor, which drives the company's workstations and servers.

But it is for masterminding the transformation of an obscure programming language into the software phenomenon Java that he is perhaps best known. That might never have happened without a conscious decision to focus on fewer projects.

Throughout the 1980s, Joy took on more and more responsibility at Sun, becoming chief scientist and director of technology. Despite his accomplishments, some aspects of the job began to niggle him. In particular, he spent too much time meeting budgets, in meetings where he wasn't needed, approving or killing projects, and refereeing turf wars.

[1] Schendler, Brent, 'The Edison of the Internet', *Fortune*, 15 February 1999.

By the end of the 1980s, the volume of projects he was involved with and the intensity of working in Silicon Valley made him hunger for a change of scene. After a brief spell in San Francisco, Joy moved to Aspen, Colorado. There he was able to minimise his direct reports and follow his whims.

The move was not without some risk. The danger was that by moving his small research team away from the 'action', he would lose touch with the decision makers back in Silicon Valley. But he decided the change was worth it.

'I concluded that you're best off away from the action sometimes', he recalls. 'It was sort of like: "do you rule in hell or serve in heaven?" '

Out in Aspen, Joy had time to really focus on the technology. A project called Oak had been developed to support interactive TV, which hadn't materialised. It was ahead of its time, but he could see its potential.

The change of scene in Aspen gave him the opportunity to focus on the language he thought could be the future of the Internet, and which became Java. The rest, as they say, is history.

As Sun's CEO Scott McNealy puts it: 'AT&T has Bell Labs, and we have Bill Joy. We get a lot more for our money.'

2. Cut out waste

Have you ever sorted through all your clothes and surprised yourself at how many you have been happy to throw out? You wonder how you could have held onto that old suit for so long? It's the same with our diaries at work. We meet people who regularly attend meetings while privately admitting they are not really needed. How often do we deliberately seek out waste? There are direct parallels between this and getting momentum going. What you can lose in one place, you gain somewhere else.

No one has done more to put this principle into practice than Julian Richer, founder of the hi-fi chain Richer Sounds. His London Bridge store is in the *Guinness Book of Records* as the most profitable sales per square foot retail site in the world. Not only is Richer brilliant at squeezing the most out of every available inch of retail space, he has institutionalised the removal of momentum barriers with a 'Cut the Crap Committee'.

The committee meets once a month and has been given free reign to remove any bureaucratic barriers that offer no tangible benefit to the company. As Julian says: 'Most companies just keep adding new systems. They never go through and clear out the obsolete ones.'

Meetings are one of the greatest devourers of managers' time. Some of our clients estimate that they spend as much as 75% of their time in meetings, only half of which are judged to be truly productive.

Do you know the type of project review meetings where the big boss is present and a cast of thousands lines up to present? You could say that these types of meetings are merely an exercise in control. You could be more charitable and say that it is good training for more junior people. Whatever. If you are serious about a creative revolution at work you have to take a sharp knife and conduct some major surgery on your meetings.

The kind of surgery we advocate is to reorganise radically how meetings work and to label clearly what sort of meeting it is. The effect of labelling is to send clear signals to staff about how to behave. Below are five types of meeting we use when in the ER world. The aim is to cut the time we spend in meetings by half, thus freeing up plenty of time to spend in the greenhouse. We dare you to try them!

Information only meetings

We have a company-wide meeting every month called the Big Meeting. We've now made this meeting 'information only'. We realised that trying to discuss things in such a huge group just wasn't working and was taking forever. The result? Mostly people seem happy about it. They know their time is being respected. The loss of debate is worth the time saved. If people want to argue a point then they do so informally outside the meeting.

Decisions only meetings

We have smaller teams attend these meetings, where the only responses allowed are 'yes' or 'no'. The effect has been much more interest in the agenda – 'what are we being asked to agree to?' Also, more conversations occur between participants before each decision only meeting.

Stand up meetings

Borrowed from the court of Queen Victoria, Stand Up Meetings cut down time spent dramatically. These meetings do not allow people to get comfortable in their chairs, enquire about each other's families or talk about last night's game. This doesn't mean they are entirely devoid of human niceties. It's just that standing up sends clear messages that we mean business here, OK!

Decide at the beginning meetings

Participants agree to make all the decisions first without discussion. They simply vote 'yes' or 'no' to each item on the agenda. What is effectively happening here is that they are making the decisions real (realness behaviour in action), then stepping back to see how they feel about the decisions that have already been made. More often than not people feel good about the decisions and only feel the need to go back and discuss maybe one or two. Unnecessary small talk has been cut out and only real issues come to the fore. The reason some seemingly innocuous points get the life debated out of them in traditional meetings is more to do with defensive reactions than the issues themselves.

Rattle and roll meetings

The insight behind this brand of meeting is that of ten agenda items only a small number are substantial. So in rattle and roll meetings we rattle through the eight or so less contentious points first – we do this at speed. We all feel good, we've made progress and can settle down to discuss properly the remaining more weighty issues.

3. Cut multidisciplinary monsters

The third way to lower momentum barriers is to cut multidisciplinary monsters. Multidisciplinary teams are a great idea – lots of freshness for people's differing perspectives. But we've also learnt that small is beautiful. Small teams move faster, tend to be braver in challenging conventional thinking, and are more rewarding to be part of.

4. Cut bar coding

Bar-coding time is the scourge of modern management; you have to free yourself from its clutches. 'Hot housing' is an antidote to the evils of bar coding time. Hot housing involves stepping out of the usual work environment altogether. It means taking the team right away from other distractions. But it's much more than an 'away day' or an 'offsite'.

Even though there is nothing new about the idea of getting out of the office and giving uninterrupted focus to your project, we find surprisingly few companies do it well.

Away with away days

Away days are the wrong tool for innovation for two reasons:

They are too short. Just a single day out of the office with a packed agenda starts to feel like bar coding on a macro scale. There is simply too much to do. Creative time cannot be packed with agenda items – too much pre-planning leaves no room to follow an idea and see where it leads you.

It is amazing how much an innovation team can achieve working in an isolated cottage in the country for two or three days. Given a big enough chunk of time you soon exhaust your agenda and this is when the magic begins. 'Agendaless conversation', especially out of the office, is guaranteed to provoke creativity. Once the agenda is exhausted and you have cleared your head, then the really new creative stuff comes out. That's when the team enters an area of creativity that is much more likely to be competitive. This is just not possible if you bar code time.

Same environment sneaks in. Often away days have so many trappings of the office that there is little to distinguish them. The same people are present, information is presented in the same way, the same hierarchies exist and laptops and mobile phones are indispensable. For some companies the away day venue is used so frequently that it feels like an office!

Hothouse havens

We advocate a creative revolution in the way we deal with creative meetings offsite and we call our revolution hot housing. Hot housing is when you take a project team well away from the office for an extended period of time to work solidly on one task. There are three tricks to successful hot housing:

1. Plan it in advance

It's hard to countenance taking three days out of the office. The solution is to take a good look at your innovation projects. Which ones do you really want to achieve? Block out between three and five days of solid diary time for you and your team. You will find that it may not be possible for six months. But do it anyway. Signal to them how important it is to you and stick to your guns.

2. Plan in freshness

Plan how you will run the session. Think about stimulus; think about the four Rs. Bring along some different people to shake things up. Make sure to bring great food and wine.

3. Make it isolated

Most of us don't get much isolation and when we do it's great. Hot housing does not include mobile phones, faxes or secret early morning office meetings. Ban them.

Summary

Children at play have an intensity and happy spontaneity. They have to be almost prised away from what they're doing and can't wait to get back to it. That's momentum.

In the business context, momentum is the management of energy. Think of it as an unreasonable urgency. You can spot a team with momentum a mile off – team members buzz with energy and excitement.

Momentum is contagious, but so is inertia. Momentum breeds high corporate self-esteem and makes people feel that anything is possible. Organisations that have it can be characterised as *can* companies. *Can't* companies lack momentum, and after a while they create a culture that is self-defeating.

Managing momentum involves taking personal responsibility for making things happen, and tilting the energy equation in your favour. You can either reduce the barriers to momentum, or boost motivation by increasing alignment.

Creating a crisis is a short-term strategy for increasing alignment. Long-term solutions involve confronting the 'hard edge of creativity', by taking stock of personal goals and motivations.

To reduce barriers to momentum: cut down the number of projects by learning to say 'no'; cut out waste, especially pointless meetings; cut out multidisciplinary monsters – keep teams small; cut bar code time – find ways to focus.

Creative Behaviour Five

Signalling

Imagine a world with no signals.
No road signs, no stop signs,
no traffic lights and no warning signs.
Life would be incredibly frustrating
with no one sure of exactly what was going on.

It's the same with creativity at work.
Unless you signal how you're working and where you're going,
then people will become lost and crash.

Is this you?

You go to meetings where some people are trying to be creative and others analytical. The meeting is a disaster!

There are times when you wish your team would stop with the ideas and start with the action.

You find yourself disappointed after you've introduced an idea to your boss and got nothing but reasons why it won't work.

You get frustrated that the people around you are not receptive to your ideas, always picking them apart.

You wish your colleagues would learn to lighten up a bit, stop being rational for five minutes and go with the flow of an idea.

'Signal: pre-arranged sign, conveying information or giving instrustions.'
Source: *Oxford English Dictionary*.

Signalling: explicit signs given to you and others which convey information enabling an appropriate creative response.
Source: ?What *If!*

Why signalling matters

You're driving down the road and you decide to change lanes. What do you do? Signal. Why? Because other drivers can't read you mind. If you make a sudden turn they are likely to collide with you. Once we've learned to drive, we signal like this without thinking. It's common sense and no one questions it.

But in a business environment we aren't taught to signal and most of us give no indication of what we're about to do. This is especially true when dealing with creativity. We switch from our normal analytical mode into creative mode without warning. No wonder, then, that our colleagues – still in analytical mode – crash into our ideas with an unwanted judgmental jolt. Signalling is vital to avoid these creative crashes.

In the previous chapters we looked at the first four behaviours of creative people – freshness, greenhousing, realness and momentum. In the next two chapters, we will talk about two different sorts of behaviours – signalling and bravery. Think of these final two behaviours as 'enablers'. They support the first four. They are the essential driving skills needed to facilitate creativity at work. If the creative process were a car, then the first three habits would be the gears. Momentum would be the throttle, which propels the process forward. Signalling involves using your indicators to avoid a pile-up. Bravery, our final creative behaviour, is the spirit of adventure – the willingness to venture out in the car in the first place.

Signalling, then, is the fifth behaviour of creative people. It is not a complicated concept. It is simply about letting the people you are working with know what you are doing and how you are thinking. It is one of the most powerful tools of creative behaviour because it helps people to align their effort. Signalling also makes the creative process explicit and legitimate. It drives individuals and teams to make conscious decisions about how they want to work, and choose at any given point to move from the creative to the analytical state. Signalling facilitates creative liberation.

In this chapter we will help you develop more awareness of the two states of business thinking and how to navigate between them. We will explain how signalling is linked to the way the brain works, requiring us to use visual, verbal and physical signals, and we will provide practical signalling tools appropriate for both one-to-one situations and large organisations.

Where you are ...
and where you're going

Signalling is exactly what the word suggests, a conscious communication skill. It helps you, your colleagues and your intended audience to prepare mentally for the interaction ahead. People who are great at signalling work in different ways. They may warn you that the idea coming up is only half formed and therefore needs a greenhouse response, not an ER response. Or that what you're being shown is a prototype to be improved, not a finished idea. They may suggest you discuss the issue while walking around the block, or they may organise a meeting off site.

You probably signal already without realising it. But becoming more conscious of signalling behaviour brings additional benefits. It allows you and the people around

you to successfully navigate between the two worlds of work.

These two worlds are the analytical decision-making world, which we have characterised as a hospital emergency room, and which, although crucial, is currently an overly dominant style of business thinking. And the creative world, a little understood and even less experienced way of being, characterised by the creative behaviours described in this book. We have seen that these two worlds do not mix together at all well. Analytical behaviour, if used in the creative world, is corrosive. On the other hand, decision-making skills without creativity produce mediocre catch-up innovation. Creative skills without good judgement lead to costly mistakes – or nothing at all (because nothing gets done).

Yet the reality of competitive innovation is that these two worlds must coexist. They must find a harmony and balance, or, more precisely, the managers of the future who wish to play their part in a creative revolution at work must find that harmony and balance of thinking and behaving styles within themselves.

Think about it: a world of work that is all ER soon gets out-innovated by fresh young competitors. A world of work, which is all creativity, literally goes off the rails. And where the two worlds clash, you have frustration – intense frustration. Good people leave. Poor performers stay and put up with it.

So, coexistence without mixing – that is the challenge. To be able to move fluidly between these two worlds, to navigate between them at the most appropriate moments, and yet at no point to confuse or mix the rules of these two worlds. This is the balance our minds must find.

Signalling, to your colleagues and just as importantly to yourself, will enable you to navigate safely between these two worlds. It will allow you to flick the mental switch in your head that says 'I'm now operating at a different level, playing a game by different rules, and I must adapt accordingly'.

At the same time, it has to convey that same message to those you are working with, so they can respond and work with you. This is the level of awareness required of those who wish to bring their creative potential to the business world.

Think of how adults interact with children. Most parents have signals that tell the child when they are playing and when they are being serious. The child learns to interpret these signals to know when playtime is over and it's time for bed. These signals perform a vital role, especially in potentially dangerous situations. (If you are a parent you will also know how terrifying it can be when children misinterpret danger signals. The way parents signal that 'the road is a dangerous place' has to be consistently interpreted by their kids.) There are parallels here with the creative process.

Without signals, business interactions become a confusing mess of mixed messages and wasted opportunities. No one knows who is in creative and who is in analytical mode. We've all experienced this.

Have you ever been in a meeting where exploration thoughts get squashed by a probing question? Conversely, have you ever pushed for a decision and been met with another round of potential options. We have seen this frustrating spiral unwind in many businesses grappling with the need to integrate creativity with their existing traditional approach.

Consider this …

James is walking to the coffee machine at 4.00 in the afternoon to take a quick break. On the way, he sees Helen working at her computer and stops to say 'hi'.

Conversation 1 – no signalling
J: Hi Helen, how are you doing?

H: OK, thanks. I'm just finishing this presentation to a production group on our new distribution strategy.

J: What time are you on stage?

H: Tomorrow morning at 10.00. I'm just trying to bring this thing to life a bit more. I don't want to just present from a computer. It's all charts and numbers and I'm sure they've heard it all before. I've got this idea of walking them around the site with the new warehouse and road layout maps – which would bring it to life.

J: Yes, interesting idea, but it's an awfully big site. I'm not sure about that, you know. What if it starts raining?

H: Yeah, that's a good thought – I suppose you're right.

J: Happy to help – look I'll catch you later, let me know how it goes. Cheers.

H: Yeah, cheers John, see you later.

Conversation 2 – with signalling
J: Hi Helen, how are you doing?

H: OK, thanks, I'm in the middle of a presentation and well, to be honest, I'm feeling pretty stressed out. (Signal 1)

J: What's up?

H: I'm on at 10.00 a.m. tomorrow. I'm presenting a new strategy only one year after this department changed it again, and I just can't bring this thing to life – it looks really dry.

J: Do you have any ideas? (Signal 2)

H: I don't want to just present from a computer. It's all charts and numbers and I'm sure they've heard it all before. I'm not sure but maybe I could walk them round the site with the new warehouse and road layout maps – which would bring it to life. I'd appreciate any builds that can help John. (Signal 3)

J: I like your idea of doing something physical. Maybe you could present the site as a model or something and demonstrate the new flow by moving things around the model.

H: Yeah, hey, that gives me a great idea. My son James has got this wooden train set – it's full of blocks and kit, I could demonstrate the flow with that.

J: Brilliant!

H: Bit scary though. I've never done anything like that before, it's making me nervous just thinking about it. (Signal 4)

J: Why not just signal that to them. Tell them how you feel. It'll help them see you (and us) as more human. I'm sure they think we're stock control robots most of the time.

H: That makes sense, I'm sure they'll appreciate the honesty.

J: OK, good luck tomorrow, if you need to bounce anything off me before 10.00, give me a call. (Final signal)

So, what's the point here?

You were probably thinking after conversation 1, 'what's wrong with that?' James was perfectly helpful and supportive. He pointed out a couple of simple common sense considerations that helped prevent Helen from embarking on a logistically ill-advised presentation idea.

Yet, in the second conversation, the outcome is quite different and, in our opinion, much more constructive. Throughout the conversation, Helen and James were both giving and picking up signals from the other and adjusting their response accordingly.

For a start, Helen stated clearly how she felt. She was stressed out – something we can all sympathise with at work. Don't dismiss a signal as simple as how you are feeling. It doesn't happen very often in most work places. When you're in work tomorrow, count how many times people actually do signal how they are feeling. Sadly, in most business cultures this is still a rarity, and yet it is one of the most basic forms of human connection and, consequently, human communication.

This signal of emotion led James to ask two open questions to understand what was happening (SUN) and see if there were any ideas he could build on (Signal 2). For her part, Helen clearly signalled that she was open to James improving the idea she already had (Signal 3).

After this there followed a quick creative build, or nurturing of new ideas (SUN). Note how James is skilled at complimenting Helen on the part of her idea he likes. He's not taking her starting idea and making it his own – he's including her in an outcome. Then, note how Helen makes a connection with her son's train set. She's excited and clearly signalling that John's contribution has helped her make the connection.

Then came another signal of emotion (Signal 4), which allowed James to come up with another practical idea – this time to use the signalling skill itself as a tool in the presentation. Finally, he signalled that he was there to support any further ideas Helen might have, i.e. 'don't forget, I'm a "SUN" kinda guy!'

The whole effect of this is very different to the earlier conversation. First time round, Helen did not clearly signal to James what is going on for her. He can only guess and, no surprises, through the veneer of professionalism he doesn't pick up that Helen wants some real help. What he offers instead is analysis (RAIN).

Helen explains her idea without really asking for any builds and consequently doesn't get any. What she does get is a sound piece of analysis on why her idea may not work. All well and good, but certainly not a creative interaction.

And this is the whole point: using signalling as a commonly shared skill can help to alter significantly the types of conversation we have. A lot of the examples used in this book are more black and white to make the point. But if you look at this example, the difference is more subtle. There was nothing 'wrong' with the inter- action in the first conversation. It's just that with extra awareness and a simple common language, the creative antennae are tickled and these two people get more out of the interaction.

Signalling, then, is about a heightened level of awareness. An honesty, openness and clarity about what you are thinking and how you are feeling. Of course we could have rerun the conversation with many different types of signal. Helen could have signalled that while she was stressed she didn't have time left to make any fundamental changes. This would have helped James with the type of advice Helen needed. Sometimes more new ideas at the last minute do more damage than good.

Helping you to navigate

Often, the key issue with one-on-one or small groups is to ensure that every-body taking part in the discussion knows whether to be in creative (explor-atory) or business (analytical) mode.

As we have said before, both are crucial to successful innovating. It's simply that if unconsciously mixed together, neither works successfully. Signalling helps you to navigate between them and, as with all navigation, it's important to know where you are.

Below you will find, as a guide, some of the most common characteristics of the business and creative world.

Business world (ER)	Creative world
Analytical	Flowing, non-judgemental
Making a decision	Staying open
Rapid	Relaxed
Serious	Fun
Closed questions	Open questions
Narrowing options for a decision	Expanding options for new ideas
Knocking ideas (critical mode)	Building ideas – make them better
Asking why?	Asking how?
Asking what?	Asking what if?

If you observe these behaviours or hear these types of question, then it is a fair indication of which world you are in at that point.

As a rough diagnostic guide, if you need a decision now, go to ER. If it is an idea you want, go to creative mode. The more you practise signalling the easier it is to move between the two worlds effortlessly.

A running commentary

One of the most important aspects of signalling is that it prompts you to monitor exactly what thinking style you're in – and adjust accordingly. One common observation about ?What *If!*'ers from those we work with is that we seem to talk as we think rather than after we have thought.

It can sometimes sound like a stream of consciousness. In traditional companies, a lot of what is being thought is left unsaid, particularly as most business people seem to value making what they say sound as if it's been 'thought through' before they speak.

The divergence between what's being said and what's going on inside our heads at work is now so recognisable that cartoonists like Scott Adams (Dilbert) and others are making a living from it. They have tuned into the comedic potential of what doesn't get said in business. It's like a parallel universe that exists silently alongside professional (our least favourite business word) talk at work.

Signalling may be re-expressed as a running commentary on your own thoughts. Not just what the thoughts are themselves, i.e. 'my idea is x', but what you're thinking and feeling around each idea. Here are a few classics:

'I'm not sure where this idea is headed but here goes …'
(I'm going to give you a stream of consciousness here and I don't even know where it's going to end up myself, so feel free to jump in.)

'Wow, this is brilliant, listen everyone, my idea is …'
(I'm really excited about this idea, even more than the ones I got excited about ten minutes ago.)

'This isn't a build on what you just said …'
(I'm not in creative mode here, I may analyse the idea.)

If you take the last phrase or piece of self-commentary, it could easily be followed by a change of course midstream. So it might sound like this:

'This isn't a build on what you just said … So, if I did force myself to build, then my idea is …'

What you are in fact hearing in this example is someone catching themselves in mid-thought. They had engaged the analytical side of their brain (as we habitually do) and course-corrected in the one stream of thought because they realised they had stopped being creative when they wished to continue.

There is a very real difference between thinking something and saying it. Every day we are bombarded by a stream of unexpressed thoughts, the accuracy and usefulness of which we rarely bother to check. The act of expressing how your thoughts are developing exposes them to your attention in a different way. You 'wake up' to what you say and remain largely unconscious of what you just think. Get into the habit of expressing your thought patterns, and you'll be more able to navigate successfully and consciously between the creative and the ER world.

Develop a language

The signalling dictionary

So now that you understand the two worlds of business you will want to start moving more flexibly between the two. Use of a running commentary is the first step to making signalling a daily habit. It will allow your meetings and conversations to develop more fluidly, allowing you almost seamlessly to get creative and then reach decisions based on that creativity. It speeds things up. It feels more dynamic – and it's great fun.

There are two key skills required for this behaviour. First, you need to be more aware of what and how you are thinking (and feeling). Second, you need to have a language for it so that you can communicate what you notice. (As we have said, this communication is aimed at yourself as much as others!) To help, we have invented a signalling dictionary. We are sure you can add to it yourself.

It's not all plain sailing. There does seem to be an instinctive human reaction against new vocabularies. Look at how the fields of, say, IT or psychotherapy have developed in the last ten years. You can probably remember a certain amount of ridicule aimed at these new concepts when they first started creeping into everyday speech. If you can't you're probably in denial. Sorry, but notice how that term has found its place in common usage.

The same will happen with creativity. Our clients often initially reject our language. ?What *If!* has its own language of creative interaction, and our signalling dictionary becomes part accepted, part ridiculed and part tailored by each of the companies we work with.

We see this as a really healthy development. It shows the company personalising a language and adopting it as its own. How do you feel about introducing a language of creativity into your business? Here are some ideas. Take the ones you like and leave what you don't.

Signals to support freshness
'That's a great idea, let's see if we can come up with another.'
'Why don't we meet in … [relevant place].'
'Let's assume our competitors have already got here.'
'If you did know the answer, what could it be?'
'How would a kid/foreigner/ant/alien look at this problem?'
'How would Ghandi/Richard Branson/Bill Gates look at this?'

Negative signals would be:
'This is the only way to do this.'
'That's been tried before.'
'That's good enough.'
'So give me the answer.' (emphasis on *'the'*, implying only one solution)
'We don't have time to mess around here.'

Signals to support greenhousing
These include the greenhousing phrases from Chapter 2:
'Brilliant …'
'Let's try it out …'
'How can we make this better …'
'My build on your idea is …'
'I'm not going to judge …'
'What I like in the idea is …'

Negative signals would be:
'But we don't have the technology.'
'How much money will it make?'
'You cannot be serious.'
'How does it fit with our corporate strategy?'
'Ha, ha, ha.'
'You must be joking.'
'What drugs are you taking?', etc.

(Incidentally, these are (nearly) all valid things to say if you're not greenhousing. But be very careful asking questions in the greenhouse! Keep them broad and open – to invite more ideas.)

Signals to support realness
'In the interests of realness I suggest we …'
'How would we make that real right now?'
'So how might that idea look?'
'Could you draw that for me?'
'I can just make up a quick prototype.'
'Let's stop talking and just try it out.'

Negative signals would include:
'Jot it down in a memo and I'll take a look.'
'Send me a report.'
'We've got to capture this in writing.'
'Email me some time.'

Signals to support momentum

'Let's do this meeting in half our usual time.'
'What if we could finish it now'.
'Let's not go home.'
'If we stop now we'll lose the buzz.'
'It's more important to keep going with this than do anything else right now.'
'I'm really excited about this.'
'I can't tell you why, but I feel that we're really onto something.'
'Let's make the decision at the start of the meeting and discuss it later.'

Negative signals include:
'Can we pick this up again next week/month?'
'When can we all get together again?'
'This can wait.'
'Something more important has come up.'
'My secretary will call your secretary.' (Or if you are Italian, *'My people will talk to your people'.*)

Signals to support signalling

Sometimes we signal to someone that we are about to signal ...
'I'm signalling here ...'
'I just want to signal that ...'
'My signal to you would be ...'

Negative signals are:
'I haven't got time for that signalling rubbish, I'm busy.'

Signals to support bravery

'I'm outside my comfort zone here, but ...'

'This is making me really nervous, but let's do it anyway.'

'I've got that knot in my stomach again ...'

'I don't like doing that, so it's probably a good reason why I should.'

'John, you're looking uncomfortable with this ...'

'We know it makes you nervous and that's why we've asked you to have a go.'

Negative signals would be:

'You don't want to do that.'

I could do this job standing on my head.'

'Don't come running to me when it goes wrong.'

'On your head be it.'

'Don't say I didn't warn you.'

Have you any idea how dangerous this is?'

Beyond language

So far we have looked at the importance of signalling in avoiding a creative collision. We have seen how a little extra awareness can help you get so much more out of each potential creative interaction, and how it is as important to do this for yourself as it is for those around you. We have also given you a starter pack of signalling language that you can adapt to your own needs.

To help you understand the full power of signalling, we are going to explain how the brain responds to different signals. Armed with this knowledge, we think you will enjoy the practical steps that follow even more. In the realness chapter we highlighted the way people absorb information in three basic ways: verbal – taking in words and writing; visual – via pictures, diagrams and physical objects; and kinaesthetic – via action, doing and feeling. The important point is simply to ac-

knowledge that in any given audience there will be a mixture of all three, and that if you just use words, then you are likely to leave a fair percentage of your audience distinctly underwhelmed.

Now, if you think specifically about the behaviour of signalling, with its focus on helping you and others to make an appropriate response, you can see how communicating with a varied style – visual, verbal and kinaesthetic – is vital to getting the optimum reaction. So in what follows we have demonstrated the power of signals which are, at times, environmental, at times doing and at times language based. A range of powerful signals, whoever the intended audience.

Brain states

The human brain actually works in a different way in the ER world and the creative world. The speed of the brain's electrical activity causes it to act in different ways.

Four different speeds have been identified. The two slowest are Delta (deep sleep) which is great for healing (coma-state) and Theta (meditation and dreaming). Neither of these are particularly common work-states for most of us!

Of the two faster ones, Beta is the brain speed which we spend most of our time in. It's the fastest speed and enables us to multitask. Remember bar coding time? That's Beta-state in action! It's great for getting things done and ticking boxes, but not the only or indeed best state for having ideas.

This is where Alpha-state comes in. Slower than Beta, it is characterised by single focus and relaxation. Repetitive tasks that require focus on one thing are great for this. Have you ever wondered why you have your best ideas while you are driving, walking, chopping carrots, fishing or walking the dog? Put very simply, these basic tasks occupy the conscious mind, the brain waves slow down, and the subconscious mind opens up to a world of new connections you could never have predicted. (An estimated 85% of our brain power remains in our subconscious!)

So right down at this physiological level, you can signal to your brain what state you wish to attain. Just as monks attain Theta-state by deliberately controlling breathing and body function, so creatives attain Alpha-state by deliberately using techniques of simple focus – a walk round the block, relax in a chair, read a paper, tap a pencil, chew gum – they all work. The more relaxed brainstorm session is the modern business equivalent of Newton under a tree. Relaxing yourself and your team, and sending signals to help relax, is an important part of the creative's armoury.

Signals all around

In one-to-one or small groups, developing simple rules and a fluid signalling language is fine. But when we are talking about a business culture locked in the ER world, then much bigger signals are required to force people to acknowledge that the world has changed and support the new creative behaviours.

We call this the Gillette principle. To us the people at Gillette are masters at signalling change each time they develop a new razor. So, for instance, with the launch of the Gillette Mach 3 (a razor with a special suspension system for the blades) Gillette did not just redesign the blades, they redesigned the whole razor. The result was a very sexy new piece of kit, with eye-catching silver razor, go faster rubber grips, a beautiful modern pack, lots of advertising and to top it all a new name: 'Mach 3'. The razor-buying public was in no doubt that the world had moved on.

What the Gillette example illustrates is the need for much more visible, public signals to support the change. There are parallels here with an internal marketing campaign which symbolises and signals creative change.

One of the most commonly shared characteristics of creative companies is their ability to develop fixed or structural signals. These act as a permanent way of signalling to people when creativity is important. Often, they are associated with strong and visionary leadership. Fixed signals go beyond language signals and will often materially affect the feel of the working environment. These sorts of signals are great fun to create. They symbolise the fact that creativity is alive and well in your organisation and change what can sometimes feel like an abstract subject into something much more concrete.

Asda

The Asda retail business recently acquired by Wal-Mart is one of the 'big four' British retailers. In the early 1990s a stagnant business was reinvigorated by the charismatic new leader, Archie Norman. A characteristic of his style was the clear signalling to staff about how they were expected to behave. Here are some of the cultural signals he instituted:

1. **The 'Tell Archie' campaign.** Anybody in the business will get an audience with the CEO if they have an idea to improve the business. 'Tell Archie' stickers with his face were posted around the business.

   Signal: ideas are important around here, from anyone.

2. **Red Hat policy.** Every manager is encouraged to think for at least two hours each day, undisturbed. This is signalled by the display of a red hat.

   Signal: we value real thinking, not mindless 'busyness'.

3. **The Kitchen.** The building of a kitchen slap-bang in the middle of the marketing department.

   Signal: we are a food business, so let's make food (a great signal for realness behaviour).

Each structure was a definitive signal for new innovative behaviours.

The result of the initiatives at Asda was sheer magic, as anyone who visited the company will tell you. The organisation was re-energised. You could feel the buzz of the place in the reception rooms, and sense the excitement in the air. You just knew it was a business that cared about releasing creative potential.

One of the most commonly misused signals in business is the 'Away Day' or 'Offsite'. The idea is to signal creative behaviour because all the things you associate with work do not surround you. Unfortunately, people frequently bring along mobile phones, PCs and all their bad ER behaviour. Agendas get packed, the environment feels more like an office. The real signal is nothing's changed. So beware – you could be wasting your money on 'Away Days' unless you deploy the creative behaviours outlined in previous chapters.

On a more inspiring note, we have seen many examples of leaders and whole teams inventing powerful fixed signals. These include weekly 'Ideas Clinics' with no agenda. A 'Consumer Buddies' scheme where members of an R&D department buddied up with a consumer, to keep them 'real', connected to the real world. A yearly '80:20 Day' where a department cuts 20% of it's workload to create space for new work. These are all unmissable signals of what is important in these businesses.

Some of our favourite signalling structures include:

**HHCL
(leading UK advertising agency)**

Continuous use of signals to support new behaviours. Includes stand up meeting rooms for quick decisions; a double row of desks close to the entrance to force people to bump into each other; and a big push against internal memos to force people to talk.

The campus – Microsoft

Talk to someone in Microsoft about their offices in Seattle and they talk about a campus not an HQ. The site is named and built along the lines of a university and provides far more than just office facilities. The signal is clear. We're not just another business. We value the development of ideas and working differently.

The gallery – Southwest Airlines

We love the way SWA cover the walls of their reception with thousands of pictures of teams celebrating smart ideas and customer service. The signal to staff is 'we have a creative history. Today another picture will go up because we have a creative present. And tomorrow …'

Role models matter. At SWA, the company celebrates heroes at every level. At the top of the organisation, Herb Kelleher radiates inspiration. Leading by example makes a big difference. Too often we see the leaders in a company do lots of preaching but very little practising. This sends a very different signal: creative change is not so important that the leaders need to change. People like Herb Kelleher are the true pioneers, people who back words with actions and signal that creative revolution is taken seriously across the whole company.

Signalling and the creative process

The final aspect of signalling we would like to explore is advanced level signalling. It relates to an awareness of the status of ideas within the creative process. You may remember from the greenhousing chapter how ideas have a life span themselves – starting small and simple (as one-level bungalows) and growing over time as people build and conceptualise from this initial low platform (to develop skyscrapers).

An experienced creative facilitator will be able to judge the relative health of an idea, its uniqueness and its fit with the objectives of the business, and guide the conversation using the appropriate signals. Too often in creative sessions, people move on to the next idea before they have fully developed the idea that's on the table. The process can feel like a ping-pong of separate, non-connected ideas. Participants revel in the free-flow of thought and enthusiastically offer their next idea, without trying to build on the previous contribution. This is undisciplined creativity.

At the end of such sessions, the group or team is often left with a long list of ideas that have little or no practical use. This is because they are not fully developed. In fact there was little point in the group coming together – they could just as easily have downloaded their thoughts via email to the facilitator.

With advanced level signalling, you can come away from your creative interactions with a few well-built ideas, rather than a whole series of starting platforms that need further work.

Signalling

The facilitator uses signals to direct the creative energy towards building on the idea that has just been offered. Key signals from the facilitator at this stage are:

'Lets just stick with this idea – how can we make it better?'

'I want us all to push on this – even though we may all feel exhausted.'

'What do we like about this idea?'

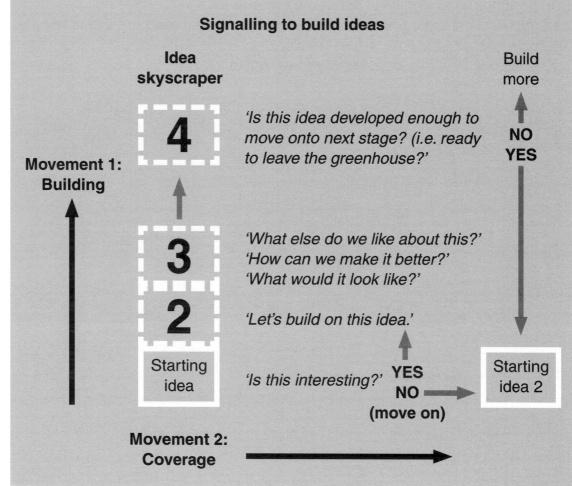

Signalling to build ideas

Idea
skyscraper

Build
more

4

'Is this idea developed enough to
move onto next stage? (i.e. ready
to leave the greenhouse?'

NO
YES

Movement 1:
Building

3

'What else do we like about this?'
'How can we make it better?'
'What would it look like?'

2

'Let's build on this idea.'

Starting
idea

'Is this interesting?' **YES**
NO
(move on)

Starting
idea 2

Movement 2:
Coverage

The skill of the facilitator is knowing which movement is most appropriate to the
flow of creative thought. In common practice, creative sessions suffer from too
much lateral movement (coverage) and not enough vertical movement (building).

De Bono's thinking hats

Edward De Bono, inventor of lateral thinking and a whole host of other creative techniques, developed another application of the signalling principle – Six Thinking Hats.

His argument is that too often we try to do all the thinking at the same time. We look at the facts of the matter, build up logical arguments, express our feelings and make decisions almost simultaneously. The result is that we can get confused or that one approach may dominate others.

The Six Thinking Hats is a method for doing one sort of thinking at a time. Instead of trying everything at once the principle is that only one hat is worn at a time. The six coloured hats represent six types of thinking.

White Hat: Facts, figures and information. What information do we have? What do we need?

Red Hat: Emotions, feelings, hunches and intuition. What do I feel about this right now?

Black Hat: Caution, truth, judgement, fitting the facts. Does this fit the facts? Will it work? Is it safe? Can it be done?

Yellow Hat: Advantages, benefits, savings. Why it can be done. Why there are benefits. Why it is good to do.

Green Hat: Exploration, proposals, suggestions, new ideas. Alternatives for action. What can we do here? Are there some different ideas?

Blue Hat: Thinking about thinking. Control of the thinking process. Summary of where we are now. Setting next step, programme of thinking.

De Bono refers to the hats as an 'attention-directing' tool because it directs our attention towards certain aspects and towards certain types of thinking. For example, when in red hat pay attention to your feelings. The hats enable us to direct attention to our style of thinking at any given moment in time.

'I'm putting on my black hat to point out what's wrong with the idea.'

or

'Let's try three minutes of Green Hat thinking, do you agree?'

By putting on the hats participants are signalling their state of mind and the style of interaction required. The hats are another example of how a simple set of signals can provide a powerful ally to creative thinking.

De Bono, Edward, *Six Thinking Hats: An Essential Approach to Business Management from the Creator of Lateral Thinking*, Little, Brown & Co., 1986.

Summary

We all recognise that signals are invaluable outside of work. But in business, we rarely signal to each other what we're thinking or about to say. As a result, people in one thinking mode can easily collide with people in another. Even where no real damage is done, the quality of interaction is not as good as it could be.

Signalling is an enabling habit that allows you to navigate between the two worlds of analysis (ER) and creativity (greenhouse) without crashing into each other.

In the business world, signalling involves creating a language where none currently exists. This allows you to provide a running commentary on your thoughts and feelings. In this way, other people can better understand the thinking mode you're in, and can be supportive. Equally importantly, you are sending conscious signals to yourself of where you are, reinforcing your own helpful behaviours.

Fixed signals – structures put in place by leaders – can provide a strong foundation for signalling in the organisational culture. To obtain the full benefits, however, requires the development of more fluid signals. A powerful tool is the introduction of a new language.

But be aware, organisational cultures have a natural resistance to the imposition of language. The best signals are those that have been customised – and personalised – by the people using them. This takes time, but means the signalling language becomes embedded in the culture.

Combining the art of signalling with an awareness of the creative process – i.e. building skyscraper ideas – is part of the art of the creative facilitator.

Creative Behaviour Six

Bravery

Right this minute, as you read this book,
somewhere in the world, there is a business meeting
where most people in the room know
that the real issue is not being dealt with,
but remain silent.

Is this you?

You walk out of a meeting thinking of three things you wish you'd said.

You rarely feel butterflies in your stomach, that nervous feeling you get when you try something new.

You pride yourself on being a careful decision maker: you always weigh up the pros and cons before making your mind up.

You sometimes wonder if this is what you were really sent here to do.

If you ignored your own prospects for promotion and acted on your instinct, you'd start making very different decisions.

Brave: Able or ready to face and endure danger or pain.
Source: *Oxford English Dictionary*

Creative Bravery: 'Creative people always take two steps into the dark. It's the always not the two steps that's important.'
Source: unknown (a ?What *If!* favourite).

Bravery at work

There is something about the concept of bravery. It fascinates and enthrals us. People who possess it in business carry a talismanic power. The Bransons, Gates, Jobs, and Roddicks of this world inspire us with their ability to jump in with both feet and do what many of us would only dream of doing, seemingly regardless of the risks.

Most of us would intuitively accept that bravery is one of the magical ingredients in the make-up of great business leaders, and great businesses. Often it is a moment of bravery, a mould-breaking step, that becomes the landmark of a celebrated business career, or the turnaround point for emerging and established businesses alike. Think of your own favourite success stories. Did any of your heroes do what they did without being brave? Highly unlikely. Think again and

notice if that act was also driven by an innovative approach at some level. The answer will nearly always be 'yes'.

Creativity and bravery have long been soul mates. Even at the most simple level, a new idea represents a new connection, something that hasn't been put together before. It requires the creative person to stand up and dare to be different. By its very nature a new idea goes against the flow of what has come before. That is what is unique about the creative act and why bravery plays such a key role.

Given its obvious importance to business success, we are intrigued by how little has been written about the subject of bravery at work. A search on the Internet or in a dictionary points you in the direction of 'risk'. There is a lot of material on the subject of risk avoidance, risk analysis and risk management. These are broadly accepted terms in everyday business vocabulary, and important too. But to spend so much effort thinking about risk management and so little, if any, on the topic of bravery, appears to us overly negative. It's like going in to a bookstore to buy *The Joy of Sex* and being told there's nothing on the subject, but 20 different books on reducing impotence.

So what of bravery in business? We don't have all the answers, but we do believe that bravery is a subject worthy of further investigation. Here we've tried to make a start.

In this chapter we focus on the paradoxical nature of bravery. Why is it that we so admire this trait in others but find it hard to be brave ourselves? Why do those who are brave rarely consider themselves to be? We also look at the barriers to bravery and how can we start to overcome them.

'There is microscopically fine line between being brilliantly creative and acting like the most gigantic idiot on earth. So what the hell, leap!'
Cynthia Heimel

Corporate bravery

Traditionally, at a corporate level, bravery relates to those decisions that carry a greater potential risk than a number of considered alternatives. Business bravery is a calculated risk, then, where the potential gain of a bolder move is considered to outweigh the benefits of a smaller, more predictable advantage.

The process is relatively simple. Imagine a pair of scales. The benefits of a potential route are outlined clearly on one side, then the risks on the other. The debate that follows simply weighs the estimated or potential gain against the downside or potential risk.

Risk assessment is a smart, analytical process to get you to a more informed position. Once you've completed a thorough risk assessment you have, supposedly, more facts on which to make a decision. However, someone somewhere has still got to put their head above the parapet and say, 'OK, let's do it'. Also you still have to cross the Rubicon, to make that bold move. Risk assessment helps us make more informed judgements at work but is doesn't explain the nature of the brave act itself.

In weighing up consequences we often allow the negative points to overwhelm the positive. Dwelling too long over a decision firms up in our mind a picture of what could go wrong. The downsides are often clear whereas we cannot 'see' the benefits of a bold new idea as clearly. Risk assessment would probably never have led Henry Ford to build a car or the Wrights to design a plane. The point is that the creative process takes a baby of an idea and, with time, blood, sweat and tears, turns it into an adult. What is seen at the beginning often bears no resemblance to what you get at the end. The potential, the magic, the unmeasurable in a great idea is easily missed in risk assessment.

Personal bravery

At a personal level, brave people at work are usually those who are willing to speak their mind. When we ask businesses to identify who their bravest souls are, they usually respond in one of three ways:

1. The person, typically with a high level of power, who has stuck his or her neck out and made a bold decision that they take responsibility for.

2. The person in meetings who is not afraid to speak their mind regardless of the 'flow of consensus'.

3. The talented maverick who has settled in the organisation and is considered to be somewhat unpromotable due to the unorthodoxy of their views, and their inability to be 'appropriately pragmatic' with them.

These are the commonly held perceptions of personal bravery at work today. There are some useful insights to be gleaned from this, but perhaps the most intriguing aspect is that nearly everyone considers bravery to be an almost genetic quality. He or she is brave, he or she has brown eyes. Never, 'well, Jay used to be a mouse, but he roars like a tiger in meetings now'. For most people, bravery is something you've either got or you haven't got. We disagree.

Bravery is not a genetic quality. In business, you cannot simply explain bravery in terms of risk. Risk assessment is just the warm-up – bravery is the race.

'The greatest mistake you can make in life is to be continually fearing you will make one.'
Albert G. Hubbard

213

A re-expression of bravery

We don't accept that bravery is an innate quality. We think it's something you can practise upon and improve, and what's more, that you can structure it into your business life.

The original meaning of the word 'courage' is 'to speak your mind with all your heart'. Did you notice the sort of people referred to earlier as the most commonly perceived to be 'brave'? There is something that unites the ballsy leader, the outspoken and the maverick, some quality of self. The origins of bravery are profoundly intimate. They are about being true to yourself.

The current myth of bravery is that some acts are 'brave' while others are not, yet the reality is that this is only the perception of the onlooker. Those who are classified as brave typically do not recognise their own bravery. This is a crucial point. They were not setting out to be brave, and often disclaim the act in these terms. 'I had no choice' or 'I just set out to do what I knew I had to do'. Bravery is the label of the onlooker but not the intention of the principal involved.

Try this theory out for yourself. Ask several entrepreneurs who you believe to have shown great bravery whether they consider themselves to be unusually brave. Very few of them will answer yes. More often they will simply describe a situation where they felt they had no choice but to act as they did. This is certainly true for us at ?What *If!* When we first left our comfortable corporate jobs for a minimal wage and a single Apple Mac, people thought we were showing extraordinary bravery. They kept slapping us on the back and saying 'Good luck guys, I wish I had your balls!' It wasn't like that for us. We simply had to live our dreams. We had always believed we would run our own business and the time had come.

We weren't being brave, we simply felt we had no choice. We didn't understand why others kept calling us brave.

In our view, then, bravery is entirely relative. Its source lies deep within ourselves, not by comparison with others. For this reason, bravery is accessible to all. It is the habit of those who know who they are and remain true to that vision. A habit of staying true, of integrity, which grows with the brave.

For this reason, bravery is the great leveller. 'Fortune favours the brave' as the saying goes. How often have you read a biographer talk down any claim to exceptional talents within his subject? Our history books are full of men and women whose distinguishing feature was their self-truth, not their talent. Bravery raises the averagely talented to a life of real achievement – business, personal and spiritual.

In a creative sense, bravery is the behaviour that engages all the others in this book and it is fitting that it should end our call to arms for a creative revolution at work. It is the behaviour that provides the spark that ignites the creative flame.

'People cannot discover new oceans, until they have the courage to lose sight of the shore.'

Anon.

Creativity and bravery

The simple fact is that it takes guts to be creative. A new idea requires the creative person to stand up and say 'this is me, this is the product of my thinking, of who I am'. There is a fine line between feeling that you could say something brilliant or make a fool of yourself. A new idea goes against the flow of what has come before. That is its uniqueness. That is the creative act.

So even at this most basic level, creativity requires integrity. For some of us who are used to having ideas, this may seem like something of an overstatement. Often, though, creative integrity is lacking in business situations. At work, many of us subconsciously prefer not to push too hard. We hold back from truly letting go and releasing our whole unique selves into the creative process. We monitor the relative acceptability of our ideas and hold back the more off-the-wall thoughts in fear of judgement. It takes real strength to just let the connections of the mind pour forth. It is very self-exposing, and yet this progression to more radical creativity is the essence of bravery.

If you want to try an exercise to illustrate this point, get a small group of colleagues together in a circle and place an object, any object, in the middle. The purpose of the game is to mime using the object, until someone gets it. You then put the object down, and the next person, not necessarily the one who guessed right, then steps in. Play for 10 minutes and allow silence and inactivity, if it comes.

What you will discover is that some people step forward more readily than others. The ones who hold back are caught in the headlight of their fears (more on this later). Yet even the ones who step forward will produce mimes that are typically very obvious, taking just a split second to guess. They, in turn, are caught in the fear of miming in full view with nobody getting it. Lead a discussion with the group and you will probably find that most people thought of something much more obtuse and off the wall but didn't dare do it.

Now go back to the game. Change the rules. Ask people to step into the middle without a thought of what they are going to do – to pick up the object and just go with it. This requires true spontaneous creativity – a free flow of connection. The game will move a lot slower than before, as people struggle to let go of their need to plan, to quickly assess the 'suitability' of an idea before exposing it to the world.

This simple game is highly illustrative of how creativity happens in the business world. True creativity requires us to be our true selves, to expose our true selves, and for many of us, it is much easier to play safe, to offer safe ideas that we believe will be accepted. This leads to creativity of sorts, to incrementalism. No bad thing in itself, but like grape-juice to the rich claret of true innovation.

Bravery is vital to the creative process, then, because it enables those individuals to offer the full power of their minds, their spontaneous creative connection-making, without self-censoring to mediocre acceptability. Again, this is the quality of being true to yourself, of stating what you are capable of, and having the personal integrity to know that this self-expression is what really matters most, not the judgement of others.

It is this strength of self that facilitates the other key aspect of creativity, the ability to let go of one's own view of the world and go with the flow of someone else's thinking (the 'suspend judgement' part of SUN). It sounds obvious that we are much more likely to produce a new connection if we open up to a new way of thinking. Often, it involves an approach from someone else that at first impression to us seems 'wrong' or 'wasteful' or just different (outside our own 'ideas bandwidth').

This combination of being true to yourself and yet at the same time able to let go of your own view may seem at first contradictory. But only the person who really knows who they are will be brave enough not to defend their point of view at every turn. They have the strength to let go, to be flexible. The less sure person will react like a wounded cat and pounce on your idea. The most defensive people are invariably those who are least sure of themselves – that is why they react so quickly to make themselves look strong.

Creativity, in summary, is an act which is intimately related to personal bravery, and consequently, to our own personal strength, our ability to be who we are, true to ourselves. Think again of the 'miming game' earlier on. It is a very simple example of how creativity links to our ability to confront and conquer our fears.

Most of the great business innovations have involved this letting go, leaping into the dark with that strong sense of self. When Thomas Watson Junior invested $millions in the development of the world's first commercial mainframe computer technology, for example, he did so on the hunch that there was a market for only five in the world. But he went ahead and developed it anyway.

The ability to see that business needs certainty and yet that creativity is always uncertain. Putting ideas to the test in the real world and seeing them through. Signalling to ourselves and those around us that we believe in our ideas, because we believe in ourselves. This is the importance of bravery to creativity and ultimately, to step-change innovation. So if bravery is all about simply remaining true to yourself, why do so many of us find it so hard to do?

'It is not because things are difficult that we do not dare; it is because we do not dare that things are difficult.'
Seneca

Why is bravery difficult?

This is not a personal therapy book. However, we believe that the ability to be-have bravely is intimately linked with personal strength and knowledge of self. Let's boil bravery down to its absolute essence.

You're sitting in that meeting and you know the boss is talking baloney. You know that what you have to offer this group makes more sense for the business, and you've also noticed that nobody else is saying anything. Decision time.

or

You're in a creative session, your mind has just produced this crazy but intriguing connection – should you say anything? What will people think? Decision time.

Let's dig deep into the make-up of such a decision and explore the factors that will help determine the outcome. Imagine yourself in one of the situations above, but now it's in a movie, and the movie is employing one of those freeze-frame devices where everybody else stops. You come out of your body, and discuss, Woody Allen-style, the pros and cons of the action you might take. In our version of the film, there are five key elements which make the brave step so difficult to take and, like Woody, we're going to present them before you in all their introspec-tive glory.

Barrier 1: fear

All of us are held back by our fears. They are the self-limiting beliefs which most constrain the release of our creative potential. For most of us, they were put there before we were even eight years old, yet they live on, as real as ever, whether they are relevant now or not.

Take the creative session example. What would Woody say?

'You gotta be joking, you can't say that, they'll think you're crazy, that idea is the product of a sick mind. Before the brainstorm is through the group will have reported to the CEO and there'll be a brown envelope waiting on your desk. You've gotta wife and kids to support – my God! Let's get the hell out of here!'

To some extent, we are all trapped like this in the headlight of our fears. Fear of failure, of looking stupid; fear of not being good enough, smart enough, creative enough. And all these lead to that all-encompassing human fear – rejection. Rejection from the group (our colleagues), from the family.

In short, our fears play a huge part in preventing us from performing to our true creative potential. They strangle the brave idea before it sees the light of day.

Barrier 2: knowing who you are

There are always consequences to any act, and probably more consequences with a brave act. If we accept that most of us have our own fears, what is it that stops us from choosing the path of least resistance every time, all of us acting like smooth politicians picking the most pragmatic line? The simple answer is that

'I'm a brave man trapped inside a coward's body.'

(We're not sure if Woody said this but he might have)

little something called self, or even self-esteem. It is the little jab in the mind that goads us when we leave a meeting not having said what we really meant, or spurs us to carry on with a project when all around are knocking it. This little voice of self says 'you have to do this, I cannot live with you if you don't, this is not what we stand for!'

But what if this little voice is less clear? What if it is not so sure what you do stand for, what is acceptable, what you really want in life? Then the conversation becomes more difficult. Put simply, if you're not sure who you are and how you want to behave, then the allure of the pragmatic approach will often prove too strong.

'All the significant battles are waged within the self.'
Sheldon Kopp

Self-esteem and creativity

Bravery can emerge from both high and low self-esteem. Can you think of celebrated men and women on either side? Both act bravely but from a different place.

High self-esteem	**Low self-esteem**	**Low self-esteem**
↓	↓	↓
Clear understanding of who I am	'Parts of me are just not good enough.'	'Parts of me are just not good enough.'
↓	↓	↓
Open response, much more likely to 'go with the flow' of a new idea	Defensive reaction to situations which expose perceived 'weaknesses'	Defensive reaction to situations which expose perceived 'weaknesses'
↓	↓	↓
Brave acts, which to them are simply a statement of who they are	Brave acts which prove to others that they are not weak	Pragmatic acts often avoiding painful situations
↓	↓	↓
Achieve real sustainable happiness and sense of achievement	More brave acts because the self-esteem hole cannot be plugged by other people's opinions	Create a comfort zone which becomes more fixed over time
↓	↓	↓
BRAVERY	**BRAVERY**	**FEAR**

Barrier 3: no vision

Let's go back to the meeting above where the boss is talking nonsense. You leave the meeting having said nothing, just like everybody else. 'No big deal', you tell yourself at first, but the little voice of self won't go away. 'You had something to offer, you could have made a real difference', it says. Faced with this situation, how many times have you said something along the lines of 'I should really have said this'. What we are doing in our heads is rehearsing the scene. The problem is that the scene has passed. It's too late for a rehearsal. Rehearsals work before the event. In general, very few of us are in the habit of visioning how we want to be, running things through our head, describing a clear picture of how we should react. Without this vision, our minds are confronted with a new situation without clear guidelines. In rush the fears, they don't need a rehearsal, and out pops the pragmatist!

Barrier 4: bad habits grow

We become used to not living at our full potential. In fact, being who we really could be is much scarier than staying where we currently are. Not being brave becomes a habit – ingrained in us, expected from us and by us. Occasionally we let our hair down and show our true selves, to be greeted with that painful 'I never knew you were like that!' comment. Maybe we have let ourselves become so far removed from who we really want to be that the move seems too scary. Paralysed by the scale of this change, we make no changes at all. Fear and compromise thrive in this environment. Our habits become set and we do nothing to challenge them. 'I've never challenged the boss before, so why should I start now?' Our habits become a self-fulfilling prophecy.

Barrier 5: a non-supportive environment

Everything that we are talking about here is easy to say, hard to do. No pretending, the behaviour of creative bravery is a real self-investment. Some organisational cultures make an already difficult terrain even more hazardous. They just don't encourage or support bravery. The challenge to senior management is not welcomed, the off-the-wall idea greeted with a sarcastic quip, the brave act grudgingly recognised, not celebrated and rewarded. In such environments, bravery is even more difficult. This lack of support from leadership, and from the company culture as a whole, is frequently cited by business people as their main barrier to bravery. Even so, it's not an excuse not to do it, it's just a factor that makes it harder.

So, where are we? What we have tried to do here is simply and briefly highlight the five factors that paralyse the act of bravery, and which prevent us from being all we can be, true to ourselves. These five factors, in turn, provide a framework for doing something about it – for designing your own practical Bravery Plan.

The 5 steps to creative bravery

This simple model addresses each of the five barriers in turn, and can form the basis of a personal, team and corporate bravery plan.

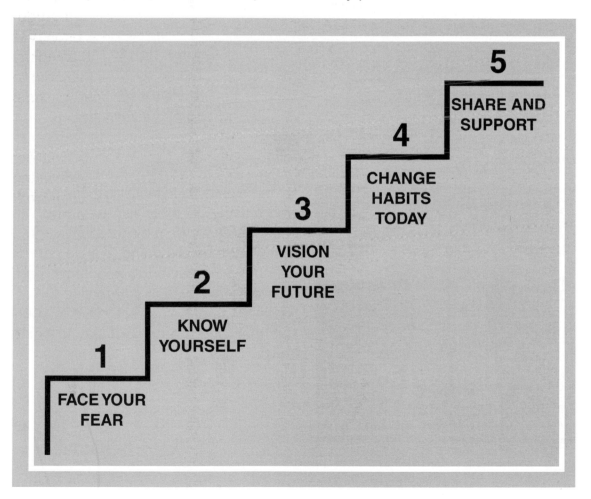

Step 1: face your fear
Realise the myth

Most of us shy away from being true to ourselves because we fear that the consequences will lead to rejection, a disconnection from the group (work, family, and friends). We act like these two forces of self-truth and connection are in conflict.

Self-truth		**Connection to the group**
'I must do my own thing even if people won't like me.'	⬅ ⬤ ➡	'I must do what people want me to do so they like me.'

Yet this is a myth. In fact, it is those people who bravely go their own way who win our admiration. We may not always agree with what they are doing, but we cannot help but be attracted to people who are true to themselves. If you realise the attractiveness of being really true to yourself, then you are on your way to being brave.

Let them out

Ever had a big worry plague your mind, then talked to a friend and felt a whole lot better? It's as though some big weight was lifted from your shoulders. Somehow a fear left unspoken grows in the mind. Left to our devices the fear can often paralyse us. Everyone can recognise this moment. The great thing is there's a very simple antidote – let those fears out!

Do a reality check. Talk about them with a friend or colleague. In our heads our fears are often overwhelming. So get them out in the open, deliberately check which of the fears are real, which are imaginary. You'll find that the vast majority are your imagination rather than reality. Act out the situation you want to face. Rehearse and practise what you want to do before you do it. It's what happens before you do a parachute jump. For a whole day you rehearse so that when the moment comes you do it automatically. You've practised living with your fears.

Imagine the worst case scenario. Sit down and go through bit by bit the worst possibility and then what you'd do if it happened. You'll often find there's a silver lining. For instance a friend of ours, Sophie, couldn't decide if she wanted to leave her prestigious director's job to join a start up. 'It could all go belly-up,' she said. When asked what that would mean she added 'well I'd be forced to go and get another job in marketing' … not such a big risk after all! Remember the mind can be a dark cupboard for our fears, so let them out.

227

Step 2: know yourself
What's your comfort zone?

Bravery is entirely relative – what is brave to you is an everyday act to someone else and vice versa. The important thing is to know where you are right now. All of us have our own particular fears that hold us back. If you want to break through this, you must start with self-awareness. We do this using a simple model.

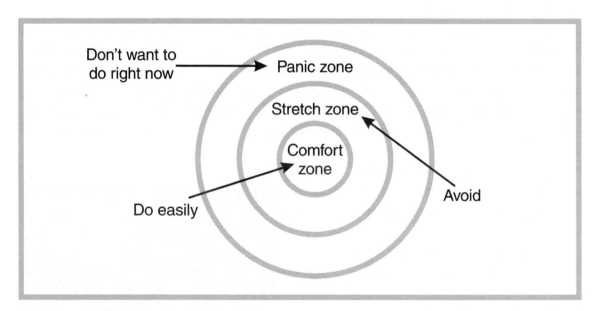

The comfort zone represents what we do most weeks in our lives without a second thought. The stretch zone is our area of personal development. We have to face one of our fears to do it. The panic zone represents things we just don't want to do. It may change in the future, but for now, no thanks. If you want some stimulus to help fill this model in, think of your work life now – the bits that you even struggle to recall are probably your comfort zone. Those moments you dread, avoid, or leave you saying, 'I wish I had', or 'I wish I could' are in your stretch zone. The panic zone is self explanatory, but don't be surprised to see yourself doing even these things in the fullness of time! Now make a pact with yourself to do at least one stretch activity per week.

Step 3: vision your future
Positive visualisation
In his fabulous best-seller, *The Road Less Travelled*, M. Scott Peck talks about the importance of attaching yourself to a vision that personally motivates you. This attachment provides the crucial motivation to step beyond your comfort zone and through your fears. Too often our fears are our focus. Visualisation is the technique of deliberately creating a picture of success, then focusing on the benefits and rewards of our efforts. It involves focusing beyond the pain to the gain.

Top sports people have been practising this for years. They work on their ability to visualise success in their minds, to actually picture themselves winning. The brain reacts to this visual image every bit as powerfully as if it were happening in real life. It has been recorded that athletes produce 'winning' hormones, just by visualising success. It's why so much of sport is referred to as a mind game; why winning the mental battle is as important as the physical and why so many sports teams and athletes have motivational coaches as well as physical ones.

You need the same at work. Visualise how you will be in a meeting or in a creative session, talking to your boss, dealing with that domineering supplier or client, etc. Visualise how you want to be, play it through in your mind, think how great it will be to act this way. In doing so, you'll create a mindset of success, a focus, which pulls you through your fears.

It has been said that we live in our fears. Visualisation provides you with the opportunity to replace fears consciously with success.

Step 4: change habits today
Start small

Sometimes people get a sudden burst of bravery like an adrenaline rush. They want to change everything overnight. This is often counterproductive. What you are trying to do is make bravery a habit, not one enormous heroic act. Think in terms of the courage and persistence to invent the light bulb rather than the charge of the Light Brigade. Start small, pick the issues that are just in your stretch zone (one little extra truth in a meeting), and build from there. Develop a bravery habit.

Change your language

Brave people focus on success. They dream it; they visualise it and they talk about it. Remember the *can* and *can't* cultures of the momentum behaviour. One of the most striking differences between these two cultures is language. Whenever we walk into a new business one of the first things we do is listen to the language. It is the lifeblood of a business – the constant chatter, which infuses the business with a sense of itself and its state of being. In a *can* business the language is of potential and possibility, it reflects a state of growth. The focus is on success. So, like the positive visualisation, it supports and motivates the individuals to be brave. In a *can't* business the language is of fear and risk. It reflects a state of stagnation. The focus is on avoidance of failure and so promotes a climate of fear.

What happens in businesses, happens in teams and happens in your head. Pay attention to what you say. Watch out for the undermining negative snipes and instead encourage the positive. Remember, what you focus on and talk about grows. Deepak Chopra describes this with a beautiful metaphor, that of imagining yourself 'wrapped in a cloak' made of the words you use about yourself.

Ride the waves
Once you get into the habit of riding small waves (and remember to start small), you can then spot and take advantage of the big waves in your company. Sit like a surfer out at sea waiting and watching for the big waves of change to sweep through your company. Moments of energy and momentum are there to be caught and ridden to the beach.

Every so often in your company's history there are times when the world is ripe for change. It might be the arrival of a new CEO, an office move, a new boss, a strategic restructuring or the like. Take full advantage of such moments, they are a wonderful opportunity for bravery. These are times when the energy and momentum of the moment can be gathered up to support you in what you want to achieve. It's a time when the culture is most open to change and when new thinking and ideas will be more likely to take a hold.

So go out and ride your wave.

Step 5: support systems

This is all about the practical steps you can take to help your culture encourage bravery. If you don't feel that you have the power to do these, then have the bravery to influence!

Share and support

When Luke Skywalker set out to do battle with Darth Vader and the Evil Empire he didn't do it alone. The Rebel Alliance, of which he became part, was a group where bravery could flourish because of a common purpose and constant sharing and support.

Too often bravery is typecast as a solitary occupation. However, the reality is very different. You may not have the captain of the fastest starship in the galaxy, a princess and a 7-foot wookie at your side, but you do need to create your own support systems.

For thoughts on what you need, why not watch *Star Wars.* Who is your Jedi master training and advising you, helping you understand when to fight and when to wait? Who are your Han and Leia, constantly at your side sharing the burden and the risks, and pulling you out the fire in times of trouble? Like the Alliance do you have the leaders who provide motivation and vision, who understand what bravery is and lead by example?

Don't get caught up in the myth of the solitary hero. It's a lot easier to be brave if you know there's someone watching out for you.

Promote bravery

That which gets rewarded, happens. We're not talking about cash, we're talking about human recognition; the love and belonging we all crave. If you want brave action (and not all of you reading this book will), then promote it. Promote it as a value in your company and talk openly about those actions that fit the value (we do!) Promote the people who display it. Look for signs of it in your recruitment procedure. For example, by asking explicitly: 'what mistakes have you learnt from most?' And don't stop at the first three prepared answers. Publicise brave success stories – look at South West Airlines Wall of Fame, a veritable living museum in honour of their bravehearts!

Learnings not mistakes

Everyone, but especially leaders, must talk about learning. Make it clear and public that things which do not work out as planned will be openly discussed, the learnings taken and made public. This should become an everyday part of your business, as inevitable as an annual planning meeting. If the organisation brushes its failures under the carpet and pretends they don't happen, a stigma grows and people feel less inclined to take a risk.

Richer Sounds, the super-successful hi-fi retailer, includes a list of the company's greatest mistakes in its induction pack for new starters – you can't get much more of a clear cultural signal than that!

A culture of learning is a seed-bed for acts of bravery.

'Some people will like me and some won't. So I might as well be myself, then at least I'll know the people who like me, like me.'
Hugh Prather

Pragmatic bravery

Our challenge to you is to take bravery out of its context of an almost mystical act and start being practical. Our creative revolution demands that bravery be treated as a business challenge like any other. We don't claim to have all the answers but we do know that our five steps have given us a way of defining bravery in practical terms and helped us make bravery much more of a habit at work.

So take the five steps and create your own bravery plan. You don't have to solve everything at once but it does give you a place to start. Remember, every single person who is true to themselves is more contented then every single person who is not.

Bravery at ?What *If!*

At one of her regular personal development reviews, one explorer confessed to hating 'confrontational situations', which she classified as 'bad news'. After some discussion, her coach decided it was definitely in her stretch zone and suggested she take on the role of recruitment.

This, she thought, would naturally place her in situations where 'bad news' had to be given. (For example, 'you haven't got the job.') This was shared with her team, and n the first few months she could be seen steeling herself for the exit interviews, talking to people in the café before going to the room and rehearsing what she wanted to say.

We were all in the know on this and gave her what support we could. She even got regular mentions on the company's values board under 'bravery'. After a while, she seemed to stop talking about these types of interview. We all guessed it was now in her comfort zone. (This story illustrates parts of steps 1, 2, 3 and 5).

Summary

Creativity is by definition closely related to bravery, because it requires the creator to share a unique, personal idea, exposing themselves to potential judgement.

Bravery is not genetic. Nor can it be explained by the business skill of risk assessment.

Brave people do not think of themselves as brave, they are merely being true to themselves. This is our re-expression of bravery, knowing yourself and acting on that vision.

The five main barriers to bravery are: fear; lack of self-knowledge; lack of self-vision; negative habits; and unsupportive environments. This latter factor demonstrates how business discourages bravery by not recognising and rewarding it.

You can develop your own bravery plan and structure it into your working life. The five steps to bravery are an antidote to the barriers above.

1. Face your fear

2. Know yourself

3. Vision your future

4. Change habits today

5. Share and support

By using the five steps you can adopt a much more practical approach to bravery, making it a daily habit.

A Call to Arms

Revolution is in the air. Many organisations have realised that the world of work is changing fast. The key dynamics of business success are becoming increasingly human factors. A new management science, or perhaps more accurately art, is emerging, and for the first time the concept of managing the human mind is being taken seriously.

This book is a call to arms for those 21st-century business pioneers whose intuition, perhaps whose business experience, has led them to the same conclusion that we've reached at ?What *If!* – namely, that creativity, human beings operating at the fullness of their potential, can create that spark of difference, of added value and uniqueness, that holds the key to sustainable business advantage in the next century.

In a world where we increasingly feed off the same milk – the same 'mind food' – competitive advantage will favour those brave souls who realise that relying on a process of incremental innovation is not enough. To out-innovate the competition we need to breathe the oxygen that is creative behaviour. Without it, talk of innovation is hollow.

This book sounds a warning to all those sitting on big market shares and sends a shining beam of encouragement to those with fewer resources. The days of relying on clever downsizing are gone. A more positive, expansionist, creative surge is required; the creativity of growth not restriction. When small groups of creative entrepreneurs capitalise their venture for hundreds of millions of dollars on a weekly basis, you know the tide of business is turning. Welcome to the 21st century. The century when business will be driven by the human mind as the predominant market factor. The revolution you can choose to be part of will see the management of human imagination as the most prized management skill.

That is what this book is all about. It is a call to those pioneers who see all too clearly how the tide of business history is turning. There is now an emerging creative community who want to shape the future. They are business people, driven by results, by the bottom line, yet what is so exciting to them about this revolution is that, perhaps for the first time on such a scale, it represents an opportunity for businesses to grow in harmony with human development. The winning business of the next century will be peopled by happy, balanced, emotionally engaged and motivated groups – all aligned to a common goal.

The six creative behaviours described in this book represent a big first step for those who wish to experience what it is to be creative in a business context. It is not a challenge to be taken lightly. There are years of work and commitment ahead for those who choose to truly master the skills contained on these pages.

For yourself, and those you lead, you should be aware of what's ahead of you: the pain and the pleasure of operating at a truly creative level at work. Forcing yourself not to do the habitual, comfortable things. Letting go of your cosy world of quick judgement, forcing an alternative view when time screams to you to move on, getting your hands dirty – creating a reality, not words. Taking responsibility for your ideas, expressing who you are and having the strength to live that vision in spite of your fears. Such behaviour requires a level of personal and group awareness that many will resist. Some may even yearn for the old days when you could leave bits or even all of yourself at home and just come in to work and fit in.

Not so with real creative engagement. Take it from us, a truly creative culture feels different. As one recent recruit to ?What *If!* said: 'It's not so much that you are encouraged to bring your whole self to work, it's that you absolutely have to, there's no middle ground'. We believe that it more than pays. The buzz of a group of people creating, producing something unique, clever, and winning. Having fun, moving faster than the competition, taking pride in the bravery of the latest move. The pleasure of feeling clear, bold, of being a leader. The tangible sense of achievement – and ideas, lots of ideas – encouraged, rewarded, built into real life and executed with a jolt of energy because they matter, because they are the ideas that help define who this group of people are, and they are passionate about them.

This is what the creative pioneers will be growing. If this vision moves you then now is the time to act, to start shaping this future. You're not alone, as the case studies in this book testify. You have our support, and we will pass on our learning and knowledge to help drive this revolution further and faster. Here are three things you can get on with.

First, start practising the creative behaviours today. Second, read this book again. It will resonate all the more strongly for your having the real experience of trying these behaviours. Third, contact us and join the creative community committed to help growing a new way of working.

The creative revolution at work has started. It's up to you whether you want to help shape it. Good luck!

www.what-if.co.uk

explorers@what-if.co.uk

Index

alignment 147–50, 169
   long-term 155–7
   short-term 151–4
Apple 160
Arthur Anderson 110
Asda 196–7
away days 167
Ayling, Robert 110

bar-coding 166
   away days
      same environment 167
      too short 167
   hot housing
      make it isolated 168
      plan in freshness 168
      plan it in advance 168
Bass 84, 122, 141, 157
Ben & Jerry's Home-made Ice Cream 45
Black and Decker Paintmate 108
BMW 144
brain
   and signalling 192–4
   structure/ability 7–13
brainstorm plan 33–7
bravery
   at work 210–11
   barriers
      bad habits grow 223
      fear 220
      knowing who you are 220–21

      no vision 223
      non-supportive environment 223
   corporate 212
   and creativity 216–18
   defined 209
   difficulties 219–24
   example 235
   learning 233
   personal 213
   pragmatic 234
   promote 232–3
   re-expression 214–15
   self-esteem 222
   steps 225
      change habits today 230–31
      face your fear 226–7
      know yourself 228–9
      support systems 232–4
      vision your future 229–30
   summary 236–7
   supporting signals 191
Brent, Schendler 161
British Airways 110
British Rail 122
Browder, Charles, quote 56

computers 29
creativity
   and bravery 216–18
   momentum as key 134
   realness 106–10

revolution 240–42
and self-esteem 222
and signalling 200–204
stimulus in/ideas out 5
use of words 102–3, 105
credit cards 98

De Bono, Edward 7, 203–4
De Maestral, George 25
Decca Records 67
decision-making 177
Disney Corporation 99
Duell, Charles H. 67
Dunlop, Sandy 143
Dyson, James 113–15

Einstein, Albert, quote 13
Emergency Room (ER) style 57–8
    blind spots 67
    culture 60–61
    and greenhousing 63–5
    roots 59

freshness
    acquisition 41
    defined 3
    examples 42–3, 44–7
    importance 4–6
    long-term 38–40
    in practice 41–2, 49
    river jumping 10–15

techniques 16–37
structure 44–7
summary 48–9
supporting signals 188
Frost, Robert, quote 40

Garrison, Greg 14–15
Goethe, Johann Wolfgang von, quote 109
greenhousing
    defined 53, 54–6
    ER style 57–61
        why they don't mix 63–5
    example 84
    fixed 82–3
    importance 57–61
    lifelong challenge 88–91
    phrase book 85–7
    pocket 83–4
    in practice 66–7
    summary 92–3
    SUN model 68–9, 81
        at work 79–80
        example 76–8
        nurturing 73–6
        in practice 88–91
        suspending judgement 70–71
        understanding 71–3
    supporting signals 188–9

Handy, Charles, quote 150
Heimel, Cynthia, quote 211

HHCL 198
hot housing 168
Hubbard, Albert G. 213

ICI 42–3
ideas 38–40, 53
    building 202
    making them work 129
    ten best phrases that kill 62
IDEO 120

Joy, Bill 161–2

Kopp, Sheldon, quote 221

Leerhsen, Charles, quote 29
loyalty 18–19

market research 124
meetings [U]see[u] waste, cutting out
Microsoft 198
momentum
    alignment 147–50
        long-term 155–7
        short-term 151, 154
    barriers
        bar coding time 142–3
        examples 141, 144, 152–4, 156–7
        growth without energy management
            136–8
        innovation rollercoaster 138–40

    split inventor syndrome 143–4
    can/can't companies 133–5
    creating 145–6
    defined 129, 130–32
    reducing barriers 158
        cut bar coding 166–8
        cut down projects 158–60
        cut multidisciplinary monsters 165
        cut out waste 162–5
        examples 160–62, 166
    summary 169
    supporting signals 190
    what it feels like 131–2

Neuro-Linguistic Programming (NLP) 103
Next 123

pattern-breaking 38–40
People's Bank 122
Peter, Tom 22
Pfeffer, Jeffrey 105
Prather, Hugh, quote 233
problem solving, and lateral thinking 10–12
Procter & Gamble 23, 156
prototyping 111–120
    examples 113–15, 116–17, 120

random links 31–2
re-expression
    alternative words 18–19
    different senses 20

Index

liquid teeth example 21
someone else's perspective 21
realness
    at home 117–18
    bring your Kirk to work 108–9
    consumers 124
    defined 97, 98
    don't think just leap 119
    encourage imperfection 118
    environment 110
    examples 98–9
    great momentum maker 107
    idea builder 106–7
    knows no limits 115–17
    looping the loop 111–13
    sharing 119
    structuring 121–3
    summary 125
    supporting signals 189
    what holds it back 100–101
    word-only zones 105
    words failure 102
        brain styles 103
        insider-speak 103
        theatre of the mind 102
related worlds 22–3
    other businesses 25
    other people with related expertise 25
    Virgin Music example 24
    wider world of science, history, nature 25
Reuters 14–15

revolution 26
    handwriting example 29
    pollution solution 30
    questions
        buy twice as much 28
        do nothing 27
        exaggerate the issue 28
        half the cost 28
        reverse the process 28
    rules 26–7
Richer, Julian 47, 163
Richer Sounds 47, 163, 233
risk assessment 212
river jumping 10–13
    example 14–15
    putting 4 Rs together 33–7
    techniques 16–18, 48
        random links 17, 31–2
        re-expression 17, 18–21
        related worlds 17, 22–5
        revolution 17, 26–30
Rover 46

Saatchi and Saatchi 122
Seneca, quote 218
signalling
    advanced level 200–204
    benefits 180–82
    beyond language 192–3
    conversation with 179–80
    conversation without 178–9

creative/analytical navigation 183–4
defined 173, 176–82
dictionary 187–8
    support bravery 191
    support freshness 188
    support greenhousing 188–9
    support momentum 190
    support realness 189
    support signalling 190
examples 196, 198–9, 203–4
Gillette principle 195
importance 174–5
as running commentary 185–7
structures 196–9
summary 205
Snapshots 76–8
Southwest Airlines 44, 71, 198
stimulus 5–6
Sun Microsystems 161–2
SUN/RAIN model 68–9
at work 79–80
examples 75, 76–8, 80
nurturing 73
    find alternatives 75–6
    make it better or 'build it' 73–4
    seek value/find an angle 74–5
in practice 88–91
summary 81, 92

suspending judgement 70–71
    understanding 71–3
Superquinn supermarkets 44
Sutton, Robert 105

TLAs 104
transistor radios 75

Unilever 46

Van den Bergh 121
Virgin Cola 152
Virgin Music 24
Voltaire, quote 20

Warner, Harry M. 67
waste, cutting out 162–4
    meetings
        decide at the beginning 165
        decisions only 164
        information only 164
        rattle and roll 165
        stand up 164
Watson, Thomas Jr 67

Yeager, Chuck, quote 29

Zanuck, Daryl F. 67

We hope you enjoy this book. Please return or
renew it by the due date. You can renew it at
www.norfolk.gov.uk/libraries or by using our free
library app. Otherwise you can phone
0344 800 8020 - please have your library card and
PIN ready. You can sign up for email reminders too.

01/11/17

NORFOLK COUNTY COUNCIL
LIBRARY AND INFORMATION SERVICE

NORFOLK ITEM

30129 079 839 636

WOMEN
WARRIORS